Rural Employment & Manpower Problems
IN CHINA

CURTIS ULLERICH

Rural Employment & Manpower Problems IN CHINA

A PUBLICATION OF THE INSTITUTE OF ASIAN AFFAIRS / HAMBURG

LONDON AND NEW YORK

A publication of the Institute of Asian Affairs, Hamburg

The Institute of Asian Affairs pursues and promotes research on contemporary Asian affairs. It cooperates with other Institutes of regional studies in Hamburg which together form the Foundation German Overseas Institute.

Opinions expressed in the publications of the Institute of Asian Affairs are the authors'. They do not necessarily reflect those of the Institute.

First published 1978 by M.E. Sharpe

Reissued 2018 by Routledge
2 Park Square, Milton Park, Abingdon, Oxon OX14 4RN
711 Third Avenue, New York, NY 10017, USA

Routledge is an imprint of the Taylor & Francis Group, an informa business

Copyright © 1979 by Taylor & Francis

No part of this book may be reprinted or reproduced or utilised in any form or by any electronic, mechanical, or other means, now known or hereafter invented, including photocopying and recording, or in any information storage or retrieval system, without permission in writing from the publishers.

Notices
No responsibility is assumed by the publisher for any injury and/or damage to persons or property as a matter of products liability, negligence or otherwise, or from any use of operation of any methods, products, instructions or ideas contained in the material herein.

Practitioners and researchers must always rely on their own experience and knowledge in evaluating and using any information, methods, compounds, or experiments described herein. In using such information or methods they should be mindful of their own safety and the safety of others, including parties for whom they have a professional responsibility.

Product or corporate names may be trademarks or registered trademarks, and are used only for identification and explanation without intent to infringe.

Publisher's Note
The publisher has gone to great lengths to ensure the quality of this reprint but points out that some imperfections in the original copies may be apparent.

Disclaimer
The publisher has made every effort to trace copyright holders and welcomes correspondence from those they have been unable to contact.

A Library of Congress record exists under LC control number: 78063607

ISBN 13: 978-0-87332-128-0 (hbk)
ISBN 13: 978-1-138-89715-1 (pbk)
ISBN 13: 978-1-315-17897-4 (ebk)

In memoriam

John   Pizurki

who knew the old Yünnanfu in its squalor
but never came to see the new Kunming.

CONTENTS

FOREWORD 9

CHAPTER I
    Introduction 11

CHAPTER II
    The Land/Labour Situation Before 1949 13
    Land 13
    Population 14
    Farm size and fragmentation 16
    Land tenure 18
    Incidences on rural employment 20

CHAPTER III
    The Communist Conception of the Labour Problem 23
    The early Communist conception of the labour problem 23
    Transition at the end of the Civil War 27

CHAPTER IV
    Stages of Rural Reform 31
    From mutuality to cooperation 31
    Incidences on employment 36
    Changes in the demographic and economic premises 40

CHAPTER V
    Labour in the People's Communes 42
    The communes as definitive solution to the rural labour problem 42
    Corrective manpower policies during the Consolidation Period 49

CHAPTER VI
    Employment Policies During the Third and Fourth Plan Periods 57
    Employment in agriculture 59
    Small-scale rural industries 64
    Mass labour schemes for capital construction 74

	Labour supply to state industry	91
	Impact on China's agriculture and food production	92
	Rural capital supply	97

CHAPTER VII

Mechanization and Future Outlook   99

	Definition of mechanization	100
	The three-stage strategy	101
	Initial Stage: Tractorization	104
	Constraints upon rapid mechanization	104
	Selective mechanization	105
	Mechanization "in the main"	111

CHAPTER VIII

Conclusions   115

BIBLIOGRAPHY   129

LIST OF TABLES

Table 1	Population and arable land	15
Table 2	Average landholding sizes in 1944	18
Table 3	Division of rural population by classes and land holdings	19
Table 4	Average labour inputs in crop cultivation 1930 and 1958	60
Table 5	Large-scale and small-scale industry, comparison	65
Table 6	China's human mass labour investment 1964-1977	81
Table 7	China's foodgrain production 1970-1976	93
Table 8	Mechanization of Chinese agriculture	106

FOREWORD

The present study is an outgrowth of the author's puzzlement with an obvious paradox: Whereas the Chinese have always stressed the importance of their agricultural revolution in human, social and political terms, the community of Western observers has been increasingly fascinated by its more technological and quantitative achievements. While a great deal has been written about these latter aspects, Chinese invitations to take a closer look at the former ones have gone largely unheeded, particularly in the more economic-oriented quarters among China-watchers. The author himself confesses his guilt of omission and commission in this respect.

The present study, which is hardly more than a beginning, is his attempt to fill this lacuna to some extent. Having tried to study for long years what the Chinese produced, how great their GDP was, it is high time for him to pay more attention to their ways of dealing with their most precious factor, man and human labour.

As there is scant literature on this side of the Chinese experiment, only little secondary source material could be used. To a large extent the author relied on his own observations on the spot, gained during several visits, on subsequent discussions with Chinese economists and agriculturalists and on perusal of Chinese publications. It is hoped that the present study will thus contribute a few suggestions to the resuming debate on the future of the small-scale farmer, not only in the Chinese context, but in the Far East and the Third World in general, by shedding some light on approaches untried elsewhere.

CHAPTER I

Introduction

During twenty-seven years of gradual but rapid independent and original evolution, the Chinese model of social and economic development has become ever more interesting. Whereas at first most outside observers doubted that China's endeavours to solve her problems of backwardness, poverty, social disorder and economic disruption could have relevance for the non-Chinese world, not only because of the magnitude of the task and the extent of the disorganization that war and civil war had left behind, but also because of the overall approach chosen - Marxist-Leninist socialism - today it is almost undisputed that China's approach deserves a good deal of attention. The reasons are threefold:

1. China has succeeded, after gradually breaking away from the Soviet model of socialist reconstruction, in making a full adaptation of what was originally an utterly foreign concept of socio-economic development which appears to work well, in integrating into it all the essential historical and modern elements of national life and production, and in coming up with a synthesis which is sui generis.
2. On her way, she has encountered problems and obstacles which are exemplary of those most nations of the Third World have to face in their struggle out of underdevelopment, inequality, and dependence and toward modernization and prosperity.
3. In the virtual absence of alternative solutions which have withstood the test of reality, her methods are prototypical for approaches which appear apt to bring about lasting increases in national production, more social justice for all classes of the population and a genuine qualitative improvement of the nation's material well-being.

The Chinese model is based on the premise that, contrary to what most other development models predicate, agriculture and rural reconstruction are the keys to the global improvement of society. Proceeding from this premise the Chinese have come up with very interesting and original answers to such key problems as capital formation in underdeveloped societies, the generation of internal surplus for investment and the replacement of what is usually the scarcest production factor, capital, by the one that is usually the most abundant, labour. These answers are the product of a highly inventive and original process of thinking and re-thinking the needs and requirements of a backward society from the standpoint of the suffering masses, not of a privileged elite. It was born not out of the acceptance of <u>a priori</u>, theoretical assumptions borrowed from societies that have attained incomparably more developed patterns of productivity and prosperity, but rather from a sober, unbiased analysis of the Chinese material and political situation, applying the methodological tools of Marxism (as witnessed by one of their earliest writings on the subject, Mao's <u>Report on the Investigation of the Peasant Movement in Hunan</u>). The responses subsequently formulated were also based on the Marxist instrumentarium. One of the more interesting items in this arsenal is the role and use of labour in changing the material and social environment, in "making the Revolution".

An assessment of the role of labour is the more important for the over-all appraisal of success or failure of the Chinese experiment as in this issue - the mobilization, motivation and efficient utilization of the "working masses", particularly of hitherto redundant rural manpower, under existing technological conditions and without waiting for the methods and fruits of mechanization and industrialization to percolate down to that level - resides one of the most interesting characteristics of the Chinese approach. In fact, it forms a major criterion for the twofold validity of Mao Tse-tung's theoretical concept of a non-capitalistic economic development strategy, aimed at an accelerated movement out of socio-economic depression into the expansion of employment, production, goods supply and national production without relying on the play of market forces; and in a more general way for his doctrine on societal behaviour and transformation without exploitation. The present study will deal mainly with the Chinese approach to the first, narrower set of problems: China's state of rural backwardness and degeneration at the time of the Communist revolution; the path of accelerated rural reconstruction, practically without foreign help; the skillful use of indigenous factors and resource mobilization; and the future prospects for this approach as the Chinese see it today.

In our conclusions we will try to draw the lessons of the Chinese experiment as the foreign observer can see them at the present stage, and then consider whether the Chinese model bears a universal message for the Third World.

CHAPTER II

The Land/Labour Situation Before 1949

When the civil war ended - an event the Chinese call "Liberation" - China was essentially an agricultural country. Of her roughly 550 million people, more than 85 % were directly dependent on agriculture or on work related to it. Roughly 80 % of total exports, more than half of government revenue, and 80 % of the light industry inputs in the narrow coastal areas were derived from agriculture.

Land

In the first half of the 20th century, China had reached the limit of the expansion of her crop areas by traditional means. Already by then, a good deal of formerly arable land, often of initially high quality, as in the Great Northern Chinese Plain, had been seriously degraded or even lost as the result of erosion, exhaustion, man-made flooding and other destructive interventions. This process had gone on for about two thousand years and had been well observed, but nothing had been undertaken to reverse or even halt it. In the last three centuries it had assumed such proportions that large areas in the lower Huangho and Yangtze basin had been almost abandoned, while subsistence agriculture had moved up into previously forested hills and mountainous areas with even poorer soils and more adverse climates, thus depressing yields and marketable volumes of produce. In earlier centuries all this had already had ominous ecological effects such as a sharp increase in the number of floods and droughts, scarcity of water in deforested areas, dust storms, increases in the incidence of pests, the silting of lowlands and estuaries, etc.

Thus, China's total arable area had been put in the 1930s [1] at a maximum of 110 to 120 million ha, whereas at the time of Liberation it had fallen to only 97.8 million

---

1) J.L. Buck, Land Utilization in China, Chicago 1937.

ha, or roughly 10 % of China's total land area. This illustrates not only the precariousness of the area basis of Chinese agriculture but also the trend in arable land availability.

Against this, there were reserves of potentially cultivable areas which had been variously estimated as amounting to 100 to 120 million ha for the whole of China (2). None of these reserves, however, were immediately available but necessitated preparatory investment in clearing, levelling and similar works, let alone the problem of legal acquisition. Most views agreed that this total reserve could be divided into one of roughly 30-35 million ha that could be brought under the plough within the short and medium term and without too many technical difficulties through conventional means available at that time in Chinese villages; and a second reserve of between 60 and 90 million ha that would require a major capital outlay and technological inputs not then available in China's rural areas. For this, it was believed, China would have eventually to seek foreign loans and technical assistance. Some of the exploratory talks during the latter part of the Second World War envisaged such large-scale foreign aid - as was seen later in the Marshall Plan for Western Europe - for a pacified and restructured China, provided certain political pre-conditions were fullfilled.

Population

In contrast to the contraction in the supply of arable land by the early 20th century, population, which had been nearly stable for almost two thousand years, began to break through all previously conceivable ceilings. Consequently, China's man/land ratio deteriorated to an extent that today is paralleled only in areas of acutest population explosions, such as the Caribbean, Mexico, Java and West Bengal and Kerala in India. Table 1 summarizes this evolution, which occurred as follows: From the second century B.C. to the end of the 16th century, China's total population fluctuated between 60 and 100 million people for roughly the same area: the country south and east of the Great Wall. Inside these borders, a shift took place: whereas in earlier times the major concentrations of population had been in the North Chinese plains north of the Yangtze and excess population had moved south into relatively unopened hill areas only sparsely populated by allogenous tribes, from the

---

2) J.Dawson, Communist China's Agriculture, New York 1970, gives various estimates made in the 1930s.

15th or 16th century onward the centre of population gravity had moved south of the Yangtze, or, to be more precise, to the south bank of the lower course of the Yangtze. South China, in its turn, approached the threshold of relative overpopulation and from the 18th century onward shed its excess population in recurring waves of emigrations to Southeast Asia.

Table 1

Population and arable land

(all figures approximate)

Year	Total arable area (in millions of ha)	Population (in millions)	Man/land ratio
8 B.C.	39	40	.975
1542	43	63	.683
1666	48	120	.400
1793	60	292	.205
1936	110	500	.220

Source: C. Ullerich, "Die chinesischen Volkskommunen seit 1960", in Geopolitik, Marburg 1967, Vol. II.

By the middle of the 19th century, this inner migration and the departure of South Chinese emigrants to the Nanyang (South Sea) areas beyond the country's boundaries had reached the limit of what was environmentally and technologically feasible for the Chinese farming population. Attempts at internal colonization of such extramural northern and western provinces as Xinjiang and Qinghai proved for the most part to be less than successes, as only few Han settlers were willing to settle permanently on those arid, cold highland plateaus of Central Asia. One last overflow valve was opened before the Boxer War when Manchuria, hitherto closed to Han migration as a settling and hunting reservation for the Manchu people, was opened to coolie labour. Within fifty years, the total population of the three Manchurian provinces rose from less than three to over fifty million. But by and large China's growing population was compelled, from the mid-1800s onward, to concentrate in the same areas of high and rising population pressure:

- the North China plains with their intensive wheat cultivation;
- the central and lower Yangtze valley with its wet rice economy, where in the estuary population density exceeded 500 persons/sq.km;
- the wheat- and rice-growing Sichuan basin, with over 600 inhabitants/sq.km;
- the lower Guangdong basin and the South China coast where densities of 400 persons and more per sq.km are frequent.

Here, almost three quarters of the total population lived and struggled for a livelihood, while even today about half of China's territory, cold, arid and mountainous, has a population density of ten or fewer persons/sq.km.

The result of this deteriorating man/land ratio was not only that demand pressure for food produced on a constant or even locally shrinking area rose steadily, but also that the increasingly intensified cultivation systems, without proper attention to soil conservation and care, impoverished the land, driving prices of arable land, and with them tenancy rents, higher and higher.

Farm size and fragmentation

This "Man-land contradiction", as the Chinese call it, was sharpened by an ever more severe fragmentation of holdings, due mainly in the first instance to traditional Chinese inheritance laws, under which holdings were divided among the male heirs in each succession. Thus, until the heyday of the Manchu dynasty it had been traditionally held that the normal size of a Chinese family farm was 64 _mou_, or 4.4 ha. This acreage a peasant family with four to five working members could easily cultivate, even if the plot was under double-cropping, as in the south. On such a holding the average labour input was about 300 work-days per year and person, and a pair of draught oxen and several pigs could be kept. For a long time, this pattern was the norm in China's rice-growing areas; in the wheat-growing zones sizes had been slightly larger, compensating for the smaller yield.

But already by the later 1800s these normal-sized holdings had begun to disappear, first in the most densely populated areas on the East China coastlands, later on in other regions where agriculture was intensive and population continued to grow. Thus, by 1930 the overall average farm size throughout China had decreased to only 2.4 ha, with 1.4 ha the average in the centre and less than one hectare in the south (3).

During his investigations between 1928 and 1933, Buck (4) found an average farm size of only 1.34 ha. A few years later, another survey (5) showed that in the north, among tenant farms, the average was 8 mou (ca. 0.6 ha), in the centre 7 mou (ca. 0.5 ha) and in the south 4 mou (ca. 0.3 ha).

Furthermore, fragmentation continued to an absurd degree; by 1946 the average Chinese farm was composed of not fewer than six different parcels, with corresponding losses in space for fencing, demarcations, access paths, etc., and in working time for the peasants obliged to rush from one plot to another (6).

This evolution had two results, equally dangerous for the farming population. First, the peasant family was no longer able to make use of all its working capacity. Some of its members went idle and had to look for work elsewhere, at least outside the planting and harvesting seasons. Furthermore, the holdings no longer permitted the keeping of draught animals, and the farmers were reduced to working the soil with their hoes instead of the plough. Their nutritional basis was narrowed because the number of pigs and poultry that could feed on the wastes of the plot was reduced. Secondly, cash income from the sale of a diminished production shrank, weakening the farmers' power of economic resistance. One or two bad harvests and they had to take the road to the village usurer, who in the 1930s took a predominant interest rate of 15 % per month which could rise to 100% in calamity years. Once the pauperized Chinese farmer was in the hands of the money-lender, his eviction was only a matter of time. A repressive tax system, with over 1,700 levies in some provinces by 1946, helped to crush the mass of small farm-owners. An additional burden was that personal debts were inheritable and actually passed from father to son, keeping millions of Chinese peasants in virtual bondage for generations.

---

3) T. Pang, Les Communes Populaires Rurales en Chine, Fribourg 1967, p.24.
4) Buck, op. cit., p. 154 et seq.
5) K.C. Chao, Agrarian Policy of the Chinese Communist Party, 1921-1959, Bombay 1960, p.50.
6) Pang, op. cit.

Land tenure

Under conditions such as these, the average size of the holdings of small and medium peasants was bound to diminish, while the estates of the more moneyed landowners expanded. Simultaneously, more and more small farmers lost their status as owners for that of tenants, later either becoming landless farm-hands or having to migrate to the cities after having first lost their land titles and then their livelihood from contract work.

Table 2 shows how by 1944 the average sizes for small and medium farms had sunk far below the former traditional average of 4.4 ha, in the first case by about 80 %, in the second by almost half. On the other hand, large peasants, who could afford to lend money, buy land from impoverished neighbours and rent it out, increased their holdings proportionately. This was all the more true of absentee landlords: family and clan organizations, military and government officials, rural money-lenders and the merchant class from the cities, who all considered investment in land more attractive and a safer hedge against inflation and other risks than investment in the country's nascent industrial sector.

Table 2

Average landholding sizes in 1944

	hectares
Small farms	0.84
Medium farms	2.66
Large farms	5.16
Landlords	17.40

Source: K.C. Chao, Agrarian Policy of the Chinese Communist Party 1921-1959, Bombay 1960, p.52.

Table 3 on page 19 shows how the distribution of landholdings changed within little more than fifteen years, and how much the gradual weakening of the small peasant-owner stratum, and the investment policies of the landowning classes, led to the rapid disintegration of the traditional agricultural structure. By 1945, it was reported, about 20 % of the rural population, 80 to 100 million people, already belonged to the landless worker class. At the same time, the aggregate rural debt in some eastern provinces exceeded the total value of arable land by two or three times, and in some districts it was much higher.

Table 3

Division of rural population by classes and land holdings

Category	Size of holding (in ha)	1934 rural households (%)	1934 cultivable land (%)	1949 rural households (%)	1949 cultivable land (%)
Poor and small peasants	under 0.7	68	22	72	10
Medium farmers	0.7 - 2.7	22	25	18	21
Large farmers	2.7	7	27	6	28
Landlords (non-farming)	4	3	26	4	41
Total		100	100	100	100

Sources:
1934: W.H. Wu, "Inquiry into Modern China's Land Problem", in Y.L. Wu, An Economic Survey of Communist China, New York 1956.
1949: K.C. Chao, Agrarian Policy of the Chinese Communist Party, 1921-1959, Bombay 1960, p.49.

As the value of land rose, rents increased. Payment could take three forms: in kind, crop shares and cash, the last being the most oppressive to the small tenant farmer, for in order to pay his rent, he first had to market his produce. In doing this, he was exposed to all sorts of speculative and exploitative pressures from the local trading class, often the same people to whom the rent was due. In 1936, the official land rent ceiling was 37.5 % of the net revenue, but this rule was seldom respected. In the late 1940s the figure most often quoted in the lower Yangtze valley was 78%, and 70 to 80% seem to have been frequent.

Incidences on rural employment

Increasingly frequently, tenant farmers were forced by their growing inability to pay rent in full or on time to accept substitute obligations in the form of labour; over time, these arrangements developed into a tacit bondage system. The farmer either worked the land of the rich peasant or landlord without salary during part of his working time or sent a member of his family to work on the landlord's farm more or less permanently as a hired hand, often without any remuneration even in kind. On some big estates with extensive tenant holdings, there were corvee-type mobilizations of the tenants.

In periods of high labour demand, the impoverished small farmers banded together to do their own as well as the landlord's field work jointly, or the landlord recruited a labour gang from among local landless farm-hands. Frequently, too, dispossessed small farmers and landless villagers entered into contracts with local labour entrepreneurs who then hired them out as working parties to big landowners in need of seasonal help. Such parties would move throughout the district, doing mostly harvesting work on one estate after the other. For the landowners who, as Table 3 shows, rapidly expanded their holdings, such arrangements usually offered considerable rationalization, with concomitant increases in returns on investment. Such labour gangs (Chagong or Hegong) contributed to the accentuation of class distinctions and antagonisms.

Against this background stand the increases in hidden and open unemployment: at least 20 % of the villagers had become landless and were reduced to finding their livelihood from short-term, occasional and seasonal employment if not from debt-labour. Migration of the rural depossessed to the cities was very heavy, although few figures seem to be available for the last three decades before the Communist assumption of power (6a). Female

---

6a) According to inquiries by Buck, in xian struck by flood or drought, 60% of the population in the North and 21% of that in the South had taken to migration. In the terrible famine of 1878, which had affected about 100 million people in Shanxi, Henan, Hebei, and Shandong, about 35 million had left their homes to migrate.

working capacity went largely unused or under-used. According to Buck, only 16 % of all rural workloads were carried by women, and these were mostly household chores inside the family and its compound. Simultaneously, average annual occupation among the North Chinese small farmers had sunk to roughly 100 to 120 days, and in the South it had fallen even more, to 80 to 100 days. The largest part of this newly emerging unemployment was still highly seasonal. In the 1930s Buck (7) reported from 260 villages that 81 % still had manpower shortages in the peak working periods, such as harvesting time. But at the same time there was heavy to almost total unemployment in the slack season, 80 % of which was concentrated in the four winter months between November and early March. Small and medium tenant farmers reported an average of 1.7 to 1.9 man-months, or 51 to 57 man-days, of idleness per year, mainly concentrated in the winter months. The rate was roughly the same both for the wheat and the rice areas, only one province, Sichuan, showing a significant deviation, to 0.7 man-months. These figures include only the farmers themselves, not landless labour, family members, etc., for whom the rates must have been much higher.

While China's ecologically decaying countryside was in serious need of corrective work inputs, and while food crop cultivation was stagnating, to say the least, there was on the other hand a vast army of unorganized, disoriented, unemployed labourers unable to find enough remunerative employment, if indeed it could find any at all. This in turn led to a catastrophic deterioration of nutritional standards. Hunger and undernourishment became endemic, in some areas even predominant. Millions of emarginated poor farmers died on China's country roads, as in the 1928/29 famine in the Northwest, after one single drought. Endemic hunger and famine conditions became so common that from the 1930s onward, the Kuomintang central government ceased to care about them. They were accepted facts of life.

Even if the Communists had not come to power in China, any central government that was serious about national reconstruction would have had to deal with the rural land/labour/land-fertility problem on a priority basis. In fact, contemporary history knows a number of similar endeavours, but on an infinitely smaller scale, such as the Tennessee Valley rehabilitation programme of the Rooseveltian New Deal during the 1930s, and smaller post-war schemes in Greece, Southern Italy, the Sudan, etc. Except for the American case, the results were mixed. In

---

7) Buck, op.cit., pp.30-31.

all cases, the injection of huge amounts of capital were crucial - and at that time these were not available in China and could hardly have come from the outside in sufficient volume. Moreover, existing social inequalities were not eliminated, but only alleviated at best. In Chinese conditions, on China's scale and with the considerable surplus of marginal population in areas of population pressure, it may be assumed that only a fraction of the landless rural unemployed population would have found sufficient new employment opportunities. For the remainder, conditions would have remained the same until a new crisis point was reached. This, generally speaking, is what has happened again and again in India, East and West Pakistan, Java and Sri Lanka during the last three decades. Given China's enormous plight, it was necessary to act fast, on a vast scale, comprehensively and radically. For, given the importance of the rural sector, the nation as a whole could aspire to health and restoration only if agriculture as a whole could be restabilized from its very bases and without leaving behind huge pockets of backwardness. This directly posed the problem of cultivable area and farm size if the system of individual holdings was to be maintained, the problem of technology and above all the problem of capital. In particular, this last constraint, that of inadequate financial resources, had to be lifted somehow if the two first were to be tackled successfully.

CHAPTER III

The Communist Conception of the Labour Problem

The early Communist conception of the labour problem

The Chinese Communist Party (CCP) quickly made the situation of the poor and small-peasant masses its own concern because it realized that, unlike the situation in the industrialized West and even in pre-revolutionary Russia, the rural masses did not identify themselves with bourgeois property owners but were at heart proletarians. Many Communist leaders started their careers by agitating in the rural milieu and one of the earliest surveys of the revolutionary potential inherent in the peasantry was Mao Tse-tung's Report on an Investigation of the Peasant Movement in Hunan of 1927. Furthermore, the Communists were well aware of the historical revolutionary potential of the Chinese peasantry, which often throughout Chinese history had set off decisive uprisings resulting in the overthrow of a ruling dynasty. For the CCP therefore, mobilizing the peasantry was a political question of the first order.

In classifying the various substrata of the peasantry and in distinguishing between friend and foe, the Communists largely ignored purely economic and quantitative criteria in favour of sociological and qualitative ones:

- Landlords were non-cultivating owners who derived their income solely from land rent paid by their tenants;
- Rich peasants were owners who cultivated part of their land themselves, rented part of it out, hired labour and practised money-lending;
- Medium peasants were largely farmer-owners;
- Small and poor peasants were, in the Communist terminology, subsistence farmers who rented most or all of their land from landowners and paid rent, either in cash or in kind. They, together with the landless rural proletariat, were the natural clientele of the CCP, on whom the Communist organizers relied in their work in the villages.

An effort was also made to win the medium peasants as allies, largely with the argument that if the tendencies toward concentration then at work in Chinese rural areas went unchecked, sooner or later the farmer-owners would be forced into debt, sale, tenancy and finally abandonment of their farms.

During the Jiangxi Soviets and later on in Yanan, the Communists concentrated on eliminating the landlord and rich farmer strata. Those who loaned money, charged interest, rented out land and hired labour, had considered themselves allies of the forces of law and order, i.e. the Kuomintang government, and therefore enemies of the revolutionaries and their followers in the villages, while the small peasant masses had seen in them their exploiters. Their land was confiscated and redistributed without compensation, and land debts were abolished.

The beneficiaries of this confiscation and redistribution were primarily the tenant farmers who, following the principle of "the land to those who till it!", now became owners. Where non-tenancy land remained, it was distributed to small farmers who thus increased their holdings, but only marginally, and to the landless in the villages who were thus made smallholders. On the village level, the result was a greater homogeneity of holding/ownership patterns.

Together with this land redistribution, the Communists taught the fundamentals of mutuality and cooperation. In the liberated zones they formed seasonal mutual aid organizations on a village basis, enrolling all redundant manpower in working units with a polyvalent function: to increase food production, to take on all sorts of productive work tasks, and to contribute to self-defence activities. This trend was systematized after Mao Tse-tung published his treatise Get Organized in November 1943. CCP cadres systematically studied local and traditional mutual self-help patterns, advising the farmers to restore and generalize them, slowly modifying them along political lines desired by the Party. Specifically, they taught the advantage of a first accumulation of collective capital from the proceeds of common work in the slack season, not necessarily to be distributed to each participant but to be retained for common purposes.

This action was facilitated by the fact that, apart from the more political advantages the peasants found in banding together behind the Communist flag, mutuality in working patterns had a long-standing tradition in the rural milieu. The ancient feudalist-bureaucratic order of the dynasties had heavily counted on such groupings before modern capitalistic types of landownership and tenancy had been introduced and the old organizational pattern had become obsolete. Under the Ch'ing (Manchu) dynasty, peasants had been grouped into various small units, one of which was particularly relevant: the lishe, comprising between twenty and fifty households, had been destined to organize and provide mutual aid in farm work if a family member died, fell ill or was otherwise prevented from doing the necessary work on his fields, creating a risk that the fields would go untended, the crops unharvested, and the family hungry. The baojia, much more ancient, and later on the linlu groupings, somewhat larger, had extended basic forms of cooperation under self-direction into the administrative field. The linlu headmen (laoren) accounted to the xiang (canton) magistrate for the appropriate exercise of these arrangements. More informal were such customary patterns as the dadao system in South China, under which households helped each other by lending draught animals or farm tools, gave a hand in moments of labour shortage, took over work or provided supplies in case of illness or death. Other mutual help patterns emerged under the impact of changing economic conditions. For instance, when the rapidly worsening income conditions of the 1870s and 1880s made petty thievery rampant in rural areas, farmers banded together and formed mutual nightwatch cooperatives (qing miao hui) to keep thieves away from crops and pig-sties (8). Although these social organizations had mostly collapsed during the turmoil and calamities of the civil wars and the Japanese invasion, there were still many farmers who could remember them. While the Kuomintang administration did not favour them because they could give trouble when it came to squeezing out taxes and rent, the Communists became increasingly aware of them and were certainly very much inspired by such forerunners.

In the North, the Communists observed two other informal mutual labour patterns which were unlinked to the imperial administrative system and had therefore largely survived the degenerating effects of the Manchu decline and the civil wars. The first were the small groupings based on clan and kinship bonds between families, under which related families helped each other in cases of need. Such groupings mostly worked well but were often lacking in organizational sophistication and clear, determined leadership. The other was a form of hired gangs of landless labourers, dominated by labour bosses and open to unscrupulous exploitation. The Communists gradually did away with both by giving the clan groups better leadership and by removing the press-gang chiefs and their practice of

---

8) See R.H. Myers, "Cooperation in Traditional and Modern Agriculture in China", in W.E. Willmott, ed., Economic Organization in Chinese Society, Stanford 1972, p.174, et seq.

taking cuts from the employees, and then assimilated both into newly-created labour formations of their own.

Apart from those more traditional prototypes of collective labour organization, the CCP was aware of a precedent created in the Russia of the October Revolution and the Civil War. Here, in order to break bottlenecks and make up for insufficiencies in the normal course of economic operations, all revolutionary elements had been called up to contribute voluntary, unpaid spare-time labour, the so-called <u>subbotniye</u>, "Saturday shifts". The CCP adopted this form of labour mobilization and has maintained it to the present time. For instance, the famous Ming Tomb Reservoir near Peking was largely built by <u>subbotniki</u> labour. But this type of manpower mobilization always remained supplementary and is therefore outside the scope of this study.

During the Yanan period the Communists evolved four novel patterns of labour utilization:

- the creation of big, military-style campaign bodies of full-time and part-time rural labour, reinforced by army units, party cadres and town dwellers, which <u>inter alia</u> undertook the first mass labour investment project. This, the Nanniwan scheme, under which a large wasteland area near Yanan was turned into crop fields to broaden the food base of the Communist stronghold (9), was carried out by 30 000 manual workers of all classes;
- the planned use of women in other than housework, by creating women's detachments for field work (the so-called "Large Feet", i.e. women whose feet had not been bound and who therefore were able to undertake crop work), or for inside work (the so-called "Small Feet", i.e. women with bound feet who were unable to walk far);
- the latter, along with unemployed male villagers, were organized in home work sections, thus "turning consumers into producers" and making it possible, for instance, to initiate organized cottage textile production;
- this home manufacture in turn sustained the creation of small industrial textile plants of relatively primitive technology but satisfactory output (10). Many American

---

9) The underlying theory was developed for the first time in an article in the Red Army's newspaper, <u>Jiefang Ribao</u>, Yanan, 23 Jan. 1943.
10) M.Selden, <u>The Yenan Way in Revolutionary China</u>, Cambridge, Mass.1971.

visitors had noted that Communist troops had been better dressed and shod than the KMT armies and villagers in the Communist-held Yanan area had been by and large more adequately supplied than their cousins in areas under the central government.

In this way the CCP managed to make use of available manpower in the most rational way practically possible for the moment under the constrained conditions of the Yanan exile.

Transition at the end of the Civil War

During the last stage of the Civil War and in the years immediately following the assumption of power by the Communist party, i. e. the Period of Reconstruction and Stocktaking (1949-52), the reforms tested in the Yanan days were extended to all China. The rural structure of the country was thus standardized along the following main lines:

- rural debt abolition and the expropriation of big and absentee landlords and big peasants was generalized, and the land redistributed to the rural landless;
- the instruments of these reforms were the communist Peasant Leagues, which at the time of Liberation numbered nearly one hundred million members, 30 % of whom were women. Through the Peasant Leagues, the CCP managed the confiscation of 47 million ha of arable land and three million heads of draught animals, and their redistribution to a little more than fifty million families. Impressive as this was from the psychological and social viewpoint, the average holdings of the former landless and small farmers increased only to about 0.5 to 1.3 ha, hardly a decisive step forward from the viewpoint of farm management;
- the existing peasantry was encouraged to form teams of mutual aid, pooling labour, usually of six to eight households, during the peak seasons, while otherwise individual farm enterprises remained separate and holdings and property questions were not tampered with;
- excess labour was loosely banded together for infrastructural repair and occasional utility work. It prominently mobilized the women whose working potential had been widely under-utilized.

These early, so-called democratic-socialist reforms must primarily be seen from two angles: Their first aim was to bring a modicum of social justice to the villages, and thereby to win over those segments of the peasantry which had not yet joined the Communist cause, then to eliminate all those classes who were declared or potential enemies of the new socialist order, i.e. elements "practising capitalism", by destroying their economic power basis, and thus to anchor communist political power firmly in the villages. But it should be emphasized that the Communist land reform was not a "cold" one, to use André Gunder Franck's apt terminology (10a), not a ready set of decrees handed down from the government to the villagers, but a "hot" one, kindled by revolutionary agitation at the grassroots level, using the spontaneous fervour of the rural proletariat and therefore initially displaying great regional disparities. Nor was the Chinese land reform class-neutral, e.g. by setting objective area ceilings for holdings, but it was deliberately discriminatory against landlords, who were much more thoroughly expropriated, and against rich peasants, who during the war years had been largely left untouched for political reasons and later had escaped with more lenient terms that merely curbed their economic and social power. A main objective was to force the expropriated classes off their advantageous perches and down to the level of hard physical toil along with the proletarians, so that social justice would be seen to be done and the punished elements learn the meaning of toiling for a livelihood.

Secondly, the Communists restored the people's livelihood by raising the food supply and the general living standard through increases in production. As labour was practically the only factor in immediate and abundant additional supply, it was logical - and not only ideologically correct - simply to turn mere inhabitants more and more into active participants in the production process, no matter how low their initial level of productivity.

Only after these two immediate and burning issues, land distribution and restoration of food production, had been taken care of, could the Communist government think about longer-term goals such as the "Construction of Socialism". Socialism at that time meant, following the Soviet example, industrialization above all. Agriculture was viewed as a supporting sector, the surpluses of which could be utilized to build the priority sector. Generating surpluses, however, raised the question of how to obtain them

---

10a) A.G.Franck, On Capitalist Underdevelopment, Bombay 1975, pp.68-74.

in the most rational, economical way. Here the Communists recognized quite early that, all other, mainly ideological, considerations apart, the elimination of landlords and kulaks, land distribution to the poor and landless peasants and the restoration of pre-war production levels were not enough. Maximization of surplus generation required divorcing the organizational pattern from that of existing property holdings. Unit sizes had to be brought up considerably if rational farm management and full use of manpower were to be ensured and technological innovations profitably introduced. Mechanization, the ultimate goal of a socialist agricultural production system, was unthinkable on the basis of the existing miniscule holdings.

Optimization of production unit size could be attained in three ways:

- either by letting the laws of competitive cost advantage take their way, allowing the re-emergence of a powerful, entrepreneurially dynamic class of big landowners and seeing the mass of the poor evicted. For a Communist government, this was clearly out of the question;

- or by pushing the peasantry immediately into large-scale collective units, fashioned after the Soviet kolkhoz model under state ownership, with similarly dubious consequences for production and food supply;

- or by gradually building collectives with emphasis no longer on landholding but on contributed labour, eroding step by step the significance of the property aspect and property rights up to their eventual extinction, and by offering peasants and agricultural labour, as compensation, security of income, livelihood and employment and prospects for a gradual improvement of living standards for all.

The Chinese government opted for this third approach. It proclaimed then, and has repeated ever since, that each step away from private landownership toward further collectivization would have to be accompanied, if not preceded, by corresponding progress in living standards and in the well-being of the village population, in order to convince them of the ultimate superiority of the socialist system and give them a material interest in its success. Only in this way could it hope to win the voluntary adherence of the rural population to its policy and to ensure that institutional transformation would lead to steady increases in the volume of production and not to concomitant declines in output, food supply and living standards. An adequate employment policy would play a key role in this attempt.

That such a gradual but hard-hitting land reform was politically indispensable is demonstrated by the fact that, most Chinese tenant farmers paying their rent in grain, between forty and fifty million tons of grain a year had been going into the granaries of elements that were manifest or potential political enemies of the Communist state. With such a share of the national food supply in hostile hands, it would have been easy for the opposition classes to sabotage and finally destroy the new order simply by withholding grain and provoking food shortages. It was therefore imperative to eliminate this form of non-work revenue from the distribution of national income.

This drastic appropriation of the land rent by the central State authority was again much less of a novelty in China's historical context than anti-communist observers have sought to make it appear, although it had perhaps never been carried out with such thoroughness. Japan, after the Satsuma wars, had seen a similar process. Even the French Revolution had made it a priority goal. What was perhaps new was the determined use the government made of it - although it may be argued that the Japan of the Meiji Restoration arrived by different paths at the same results.

According to Lippit's calculations (11), land rent on the eve of Liberation accounted for 26 to 30 % of agricultural income, or 17 to 20 % of national income. The Communist leadership considered that this very sizeable share, once removed from the disposable income of the hitherto landowning classes, after they had been demoted to labouring status, should not be entirely redistributed as disposable income to the poorer classes benefiting from land reform, but should be used in part for surplus accumulation and capital formation. The implementation of this policy explains the very sudden, shock-like onset of a wave of investments in the otherwise capital-poor country, which greatly astonished foreign observers in the early years of the People's Republic.

---

11) V. Lippit, <u>Land Reform and Economic Development in China</u>, White Plains, N.Y. 1975, pp. 72 <u>et seq.</u>

CHAPTER IV

Stages of Rural Reform

From mutuality to cooperation

1. Seasonal Mutual Aid Teams
As Communist power progressed from Manchuria southward in 1948-49, the local party cells and the Peasant Leagues made it one of their first concerns to seize land from the local "class enemies", redistribute it and organize the farmers into the small cooperative units which had become the backbone of agrarian structure in the liberated areas since the Yanan days: multi-family teams of seasonal mutual assistance and labour exchange. The land reform legislation of 1950 made them the basic units of village production during the interim period of political transition, and by the beginning of 1952 they had become the predominant form of organization in village production.

They united six to eight households each, but only for certain types of crop work for which, even under the traditional village structure, most Chinese farmers had sought outside help, be it from neighbours, clan relatives or hired labour gangs: for the most part ploughing, transplanting and harvesting. Otherwise the teams did not encroach upon the fundamentally private character of ownership and farm organization. Their impact on labour inputs and productivity was therefore only slightly more than marginal.

At the same time, the renting, sale and purchase of land, as well as the hiring of labour, continued, although on a much reduced scale. These surviving remnants of a capitalist economic order were not taken lightly by the political leadership. For as long as they subsisted, a return to pre-socialist patterns of the village economy was easy and probably only a matter of time and opportunity. Mere prohibitions were useless, as the leadership fully realized. Only further structural transformation of the mutual aid teams could bring lasting changes.

If the Chinese leadership sought their rapid transformation, it was therefore probably less for pressing economic reasons than for political ones. From the economic viewpoint, the transition to increasingly larger unit sizes was originally dictated by three needs: to take advantage of economies of scale, to stretch scarce skilled manpower and managerial resources, and to simplify and at the same time tighten the administrative grip on the village structure. The increases of food production brought about by the restoration of normal conditions in the countryside after the disruptions of the Civil War were apparently sufficient, but only for the moment. They gave the cities tangible proof of improvement, while the peasants were satisfied by the tax cuts and the introduction of a stable new currency that made it worth their while to deliver surpluses. It was rather the desire to do away with small-scale capitalism in the countryside and to prevent a return to "exploitative forms of production relations", i.e. the re-emergence of elements looking for private gain and therefore hostile to land reform and Communist power, that determined the leadership to push forward quickly.

The next objectives were, politically, the gradual scaling down of the pre-eminence of money and property in dealings between producers in favour of a revaluation of labour, especially of physical work; and, economically, the transition from seasonality to permanency in the functioning of the mutual aid teams, and further rationalization of the use of labour, land and tools, particularly the gradual growth of the average size of the production units.

2. Permanent Mutual Aid Teams
Mutuality, combined with the competent practical leadership provided by Communist village cadres, had convinced the peasants that collaboration with socialism had something to offer in the way of improving their incomes and their way of living. When CCP agitation made this argument the platform for calls to further steps in socialization, they followed willingly into permanent mutual aid teams. Only exceptionally did this next stage of integration enlarge the size of the production units. The emphasis was rather on the advance from seasonality to permanence in the pooling of field work and, optionally, of work animals and tools. Income was still determined by the size and yield of the individual plot, but additional revenue from higher output was distributed in the form of bonuses for extra work porportionally to labour invested.

3. Elementary Agricultural Producers' Cooperatives
This in itself was only the prelude to the first stage of a semi-socialistic production system in China's agriculture. After three years of satisfactory practice with the permanent mutual aid teams and steadily rising output - in

striking contrast to the experience during the first years of Soviet rural collectivization - the Chinese leadership felt safe in proceeding to the merger of the mutual aid teams - usually three to eight - into larger cooperatives (elementary agricultural producers' cooperatives) of twenty to fifty households. The farmers' property rights to land, work animals and tools were still respected in the letter but in practice these assets were turned over to cooperative management. In field work, the old teams subsisted as permanent groupings for common crop labour; other more sophisticated activities were now organized by the cooperative.

Hitherto, peasant income under the mutual aid team system had still been based to a large extent on rent for land and the use of tools and draught animals, but the principle of remuneration for work performed had been introduced and its part gradually widened. Now the time seemed ripe for a more fundamental revamping of the whole income system. Henceforth, labour performance was to be the predominant source of income and rent from property only a secondary and gradually disappearing factor, so that the surviving elements of capitalism in the economic order of the villages might be suppressed. However, unlike the U.S.S.R. when similar changes had been made there, the Chinese government proceeded cautiously, step by step, reviewing each advance in the light of past experience, rather than making a complete change overnight. (11a) First attempts were made to classify and standardize work functions by norms and to relate their values to each other. For this, the authorities adopted the Soviet concept of the "work-day" (trudoden), which stipulated equal and fixed rates for time and types of jobs performed. Thus, the social nature of the farmer was

---

11a) Mao himself, in his summing-up speech at the 6th expanded Plenum of the 2nd CC/CCP in September 1955, had pointed out some of the warning lessons emanating from the rural collectivization drive in the U.S.S.R. He had admonished the Party to guard itself against "Leftism" which tended to force the pace of forming collective production units. Instead, he had called for a cautious, three-pronged approach:
1. In dealing with the peasants the Party was to follow a policy of voluntarism and mutual benefit;
2. there was to be overall planning open to all and accompanied by explanations of the why and how to the masses;
3. the Party had to provide flexible guidance, never ramming through decisions.

fundamentally changed. Ceasing to be a small-scale entrepreneur, he became a worker remunerated on the basis of his labour input. Subsequently the labour-day was further broken down into ten work-points, and to each job was attributed a norm in the form of a given number of work-points for its execution. Henceforth the Chinese farmer did not earn a salary or daily or piece-work wages expressed in monetary terms, but work-points which once or twice a year are accounted against the total net gains in cash and kind from collective production; the value of the work-point is thus a variable depending to a very large extent on the quantity and quality of the collective labour input.

This system facilitated the assimilation of former landless peasants and agricultural labourers and the employment of labour teams for other than strictly agricultural tasks which the cooperatives were beginning to organize. For if there was no longer a major difference between those who owned land and those who did not, and each member's livelihood depended mainly on the amount and quality of the work he did, then it no longer really mattered what kind of work he did, whether he worked in the fields or performed ancillary duty. Everyone had gained worker status, and the cooperative had taken the first steps in assimilating agricultural production to work in industry.

Such a leveling of the rural labour force led to another highly desirable result for Chinese government planning: If all farmers now had assumed worker status, farm labour use could be planned and deployed like industrial labour. In fact, since the mid-1950s manpower, even in the countryside, has been allotted in the same way as other resources, e.g. financial resources. The Chinese Five-Year and annual plans regularly contain a sub-plan on labour utilization which is broken down and detailed at each level just as the other plan chapters are. Especially scarce manpower resources, such as doctors, engineers, agronomists, skilled technicians, teachers, veterinarians, etc. are all subject to detailed allocation under the plan. From the viewpoint of rational utilization of manpower categories in short supply, this represents a tremendous step forward, both for central planners and receiving collectives.

4. Advanced Agricultural Producers' Cooperatives

The elementary cooperatives worked so well and farmers' participation was so satisfactory that this phase needed no further extension, but could serve as a direct transition to the next step: the formation of the now fully socialist advanced agricultural producers' cooperatives. Here all producing factors such as land, animals, tools, etc., became the property of the collective. Remuneration became an exclusive function of work performed. Management was divided into three tiers; on the lowest, the work team continued to manage crop work and small-scale animal husbandry; the former elementary cooperative, now called "brigade", looked after matters of wider concern; and the new cooperative, usually comprising five to eight brigades, managed the whole.

At this stage the Chinese strategy for restructuring the organization of agricultural production had found its own methodology, which has remained unchanged ever since. New units have been created from the base, gradually reaching upward. Existing units and unit levels have never been abolished, but when the necessities of planning and organizing production so required, several smaller elements have been banded together into a new, larger unit, within which, however, they have preserved their own identity. This method of gradually superimposing new structures on a level one step higher than the highest existing one (12) has had two advantages:

First, the existing units have continued to function, and disturbances in production caused by reshuffling and unsettling individual producers and groups of peasant families have been avoided.

Secondly, the Chinese rural milieu, formerly relatively amorphous, unorganized and under-administered below the level of the ancient xiang (canton or sub-district) and only loosely controlled, even on the xiang level itself, has become administratively one of the best-structured in the entire Third World.

One first consequence of the successive integration was that territorial sizes of production units rose significantly. The average area of the seasonal mutual aid teams had been five to fifteen hectares, depending mostly on their location in the plains or in mountainous regions. For the permanent mutual aid teams it had ranged from five to thirty hectares. Elementary agricultural producers' cooperatives had grown to 20 to 300 hectares, and the advanced agricultural producers' cooperatives had again raised average unit sizes to 100 to 800 hectares. Internally, this had led to considerable rationalization, with corresponding increases in land available for cultivation. In Tachai for

---

12) The process has been analyzed in detail by B.Stavis, Making the Green Revolution, Ithaca, N.Y. 1974, p.54 et seq.

instance, the original 5,400 strips under tilling were gradually reduced to 1,700. (12a)

Incidences on employment

With the reorganization of the village structure, employment had risen considerably. According to ILO estimates (13) based on Chinese publications, the economically active population in agriculture in 1950 had amounted to 183 million people, 128 million male and 55 million female. They provided the livelihood for a rural population of 456 million persons. By 1958, the agricultural labour force had risen to approximately 239 million people, 144 million male and 95 million female. The annual increase during this period (i.e. roughly speaking, Reconstruction and the First Five-Year Plan 1952-1957) had been 3.4 %, but female employment alone was rising at nearly 8 % per annum. (Unfortunately, these very rough and aggregate figures provide no information on the intensity of employment.)

During the same period, employment in the non-agricultural sectors has risen by about 12 % or 3.5 million persons per annum, of whom the industries absorbed annually a little more than one million persons. As the total increase in the rural labour force was about 7.5 to 8 million a year, this meant that newly created non-rural jobs absorbed only a fraction of the additional manpower entering the already inflated army of job-seekers in the villages. About four to five million new labour recruits were left behind each year and had to find an occupation there. (14)

This created two dangers: first, that of an uncontrolled migration of manpower to the cities as China had witnessed it for nearly a century, especially whenever the economic situation in a rural region became tight, a natural catastrophe struck or famine was looming. In fact the industrial policy of the new government had enhanced the attraction of the cities even further by establishing, in the manufacturing and service industries, minimum wages con-

---

12a) H.W. Hsin, Tachai, Standard-bearer in Agriculture, Peking 1972, p.12.
13) ILO, Labour Force Projections 1965-1985, Asia; Geneva 1971, pp.19-74.
14) J.P. Emerson, "Employment in Mainland China", in: Economic Profile of Mainland China, Washington 1968, p.416 et seq.

siderably above the income level that even a fairly prosperous medium peasant could aspire to in his home village. As a result, and in spite of all the exhortations and brakes the administrations and the Party could apply, by 1960 about twenty million more persons had moved to urban areas than were actually needed by the industrialization process. Secondly, despite the levelling and employment-creating processes at work in the Chinese villages, there was the menace of having unemployed consumers idling in the villages indefinitely, particularly women, whom the Party had emancipated and called upon to come out and "join production". In fact, the female participation rate, which had stood at about 22 % in 1950, had climbed to 31 % and was still tending to rise.

Investigations seemed to confirm the existence of this menace. A 1956 sample survey of 539 agricultural cooperatives in five provinces showed that "average unemployment" ranged from 17 % in Jiangsu and 35 % in Sichuan to 70 % in Shanxi, although labour inputs in Shanxi and Shaanxi had attained 250 days a year for male and 120 days for female farm workers. (15) (It must be assumed that "unemployment" in this context means "not having reached this norm of work intensity".) Prime Minister Chou En-lai indirectly confirmed these views by stating that in 1956, only two thirds of the farm population had yet been productively employed. While land reform and the transition to socialism in agriculture had considerably increased production and intensified employment, then, the latter had not yet reached satisfactory levels.

In crop work itself, the situation was far from uniform. Socialization had had two effects which almost cancelled each other out, the one labour-saving, the other labour-consuming. The transition to larger management units, the cultivation of bigger plot units, rationalization through the initial use of intermediate technology, the improved organization of rural transport (16), e.g. the introduction of the wheelbarrow to supplement or replace the carrying pole, and other innovations, set free a great deal of manpower which formerly had eked out a living at near-zero productivity levels. The Twelve-Year Plan for Agricultural Development and its most prominent chapter, the Eight-Character Charter, promulgated in 1956, spelled out a great number of such early labour-saving policies, such as

---

15) Jiaoxue yu yanjin, Feb.1957, quoted in L.Orleans, "Problems of Manpower Absorption in Rural China", The China Quarterly, London, July 1961, p. 58 et seq.
16) Upon which, prior to Liberation, more than 30% of all labour inputs had been spent in some provinces.

the improvement of ploughing implements, the introduction of the spade, a general reform of hand tools, introduction of better and more rational working methods, etc. The beginning of more rational village management in the wake of the arrival of the first trained farm-management personnel, the redrawing of village and plot boundaries, etc., did a good deal more in this direction.

The opposite, labour-intensifying effect was created in the first place by the general multiplication of activity, such as the growing volume of short-distance haulage for which not only motorized traction but even draught animals were lacking and for which human puller teams were substituted. Thus, in Huangpu *xiang* in Guangdong province, the *xiang* party cells organized 51 human traction teams for pulling horse and donkey carts, ploughs and harrows, at five men per cart and plough and two per harrow (17). Other sources of rapidly and vastly increasing manpower requirements were

plant protection:
(with teams safeguarding the standing crops against birds, holding watch against night frost and if necessary, lighting fires and burning braziers);

pest eradication:
(thousands of villagers went on successive campaigns to hunt down rats, kill sparrows, swat flies);

soil improvement:
(topsoil, collected by the bucket from places where cultivation was impossible, was spread over crop fields, stones were removed from cultivated plots);

compost collecting:
(nightsoil and manure collection were publicized as patriotic functions for which work points and grain bonuses were credited);

water adduction:
(more wells were dug, treadmills and water wheels had to be turned);

there were the first attempts at dense planting, with an enormous consumption of labour in manual transplanting, "combing" of the growing stalks so that each would receive sun and air - and many other new activities.

---

17) Quoted in K.R. Walker, "Organization of Agricultural Production", in Eckstein et al., Economic Trends in Communist China, N.Y. 1964, p.399.

All this led to a situation in which, for example, some rice-growing collectives which suffered from a labour surplus and even palpable unemployment throughout large parts of the year began to experience labour shortages twice a year, in the transplanting and the harvesting seasons.

When reports of these large-scale labour utilization drives reached the outside world, the new policies were soon discounted as mere unemployment eradication programmes without great labour efficiency or economic profitability and of only near-marginal utility - in short, of more psychological than hard economic value. These judgements overlooked the fact that these very methods had been conceived in Yanan, where they had led in a short time, even if on a much smaller scale, to appreciable gains not so much in marginal labour productivity as in self-sufficiency of the isolated Communist-dominated zones, in at least basic self-sustenance of all producers (after all individuals capable of productive work had been turned into producers), and in supply security for the Red forces in the field. In these three respects, already before the end of the war the Chinese "Liberated Areas" had clearly surpassed the provinces held by the Kuomintang, provoking the respect of American observers (18) and reinforcing the political and economic force of the Communist dissidence. Many statements by the new leaders in Peking indicated that they felt that the whole of China was now in an analogous situation and that therefore similar methods were appropriate.

Here it is necessary to stress the link between manpower mobilization, intensified labour inputs and the new village structure. It was only through the latter and thanks to its effectiveness that the new policies could really be put into practice rather than remaining empty paper formulas, as in so many other developing countries at about the same time. For the team and cooperative structure, and it alone, provided the leadership with a closely-knit network of control instances that enrolled the village labour force, man by man; had personal knowledge of each individual and his daily activity or idleness; could turn out the work squads in winter or in cold weather; guaranteed food and payment; and looked after the manifold tasks of what by necessity bordered at first upon regimentation. Inversely, when natural disaster struck and setbacks occurred, as later on at the end of the Great Leap Forward, it was this cellular structure at and below the

---

18) E.g., Gen. Stillwell; see B.Tuchman, Stillwell and the American Experience in China, 1911-1945, New York 1972, p.472 et seq.

village level that held the discouraged villagers together, prevented panic migrations and got relief work going.

In addition to these efficient methods of labour control, the second fruit of the new village system was manpower planning. For the first time, planners at the provincial or xian level knew not only exactly how much labour was available, at what skill levels, etc., but to whom orders could be given in order to put the working force into action. Without the political, quasi-military discipline upheld by the cadres at the team level, this would have been impossible. Whoever has seen the gigantic fumbling and disorder in much smaller-scale labour mobilization drives, as in Egypt or India, can appreciate what the Chinese have achieved in this respect.

Changes in the demographic and economic premises

In the course of the First Five-Year Plan (1952-1957) several other, obviously unexpected, aspects of change, relevant to the restructuring of the rural world, came to light and forced themselves upon the attention of Chinese planners. The first census of the People's Republic in 1953 produced a total population figure of 583 million people, much more than anybody had expected and indicative of demographic growth rates far above those hitherto assumed. Although the First Plan had led to a 3.7 % annual growth rate for grain output and a total agricultural production growth rate of 4.5 % (19), these new findings had ominous implications. They signalled to the leadership that a much larger share than had been anticipated of the new, satisfactorily accumulating food surpluses generated by agriculture would have to be devoted to feeding the teeming masses of villagers. For if the rural population was expanding at well over 2 % per annum, plans and hopes to gain increasing amounts of foodstuffs and cashcrops for supply to industry and export in exchange for needed investment goods, were doomed: the surpluses would just not be forthcoming, China would again be confronted by the Stalinist dilemma of either starving the rural population to build industry, or safeguarding acceptable nutritional levels and foregoing modernization. Moreover, a second implication was that there was no immediate possibility of absorbing excess rural manpower simply by channeling one part into the growing industrial sector and

---

19) State Statistical Bureau, <u>Ten Great Years</u>, Peking 1960, pp.32-33.

keeping the remainder occupied with more labour-intensive field projects within the existing village framework until they, too, could gradually be absorbed by industry. The whole process of turning consumers into producers became very problematic, as the government faced the prospect of seeing China's rural economy working indefinitely at less than optimal degrees of employment, and the menace of seeing one of the Communists' most fundamental promises - elimination of unemployment - compromised by the facts, creating grave danger of political trouble.

At the same time the leadership had to accept evidence that industrialization would be a more drawn-out affair than had originally been expected, and that aid from other Communist countries was not forthcoming at the hoped-for volume but, on the contrary, had to be paid for and was declining, owing to political friction with the U.S.S.R. This left as an alternative source of capital supply only primitive socialist accumulation, i.e. the generation of more agricultural surpluses, and the Stalinist temptation of squeezing the peasant, which had already been rejected as politically unfeasible. Moreover, the precedents in the Soviet Union during the late Stalinian and early Khrushchevian periods had demonstrated that such an approach would burden the economy with a backward, unproductive farm sector which in the long run would no longer generate surpluses but itself become a consumer of surplus. Furthermore, industrialization turned out to be a much more intricate business than the leadership had at first anticipated. The experience of the First Five-Year Plan had shown that, in spite of all its successes, the rates of economic expansion would have to be increased considerably if China was, within a humanly acceptable time frame, to become a country with a relatively capable and modern economy that could guarantee each citizen a modicum of material safety and well-being.

On the other hand, China could not just forego industrialization, even for a limited period, for several compelling reasons. One was clearly defence. In view of the continuing hostility of the Western world, a weak country without its own armament base would soon fall victim to intimidation and aggression. Secondly, according to the Marxian class model, the new socialist society could only be built upon and through industry as the carrier of higher productivity and changes in the mode of production. Industry was the very prime mover of social transformation, and to forego industrialization would mean to give up socialism itself. Consequently, alternative approaches to the creation of an industrial sector, making use of China's particular factor endowment, would have to be devised.

CHAPTER V

Labour in the People's Communes

The commune as definitive solution to the rural labour problem

A first unequivocal lesson learned from the First Five-Year Plan was then that the population problem had to be solved if China was to accomplish her developmental take-off. This was ideologically not so simple, because Marxist authorities, and particularly Chairman Mao himself, had always maintained that a large and growing population was a blessing for the nation and that in a socialist society Malthus' teachings about the menace of food production lagging behind population growth had no validity. Thus, Mao had written in 1949, "A large population is a blessing. We shall be able to manage our country well even if its population still increases several times. The solution lies in increasing production. The fallacy maintained by Western capitalist economists such as Malthus asserting that the increase in food supplies must fall behind the increase in population, has not only been refuted long ago ... but disproved by the facts after the revolution of the Soviet Union and in the liberated regions of China." (20) This theoretical viewpoint has been steadfastly maintained by the Chinese and was expressed again in 1974 at the UN World Population Conference in Bucharest.

In practice, however, there was a consensus that at this juncture, rapid demographic growth had a delaying effect upon economic expansion and should be compressed as much as possible. Already during the First Plan period comprehensive measures had been initiated, and they continue without great change in emphasis until today (21).

---

20) T.T. Mao, "We Must Learn to Do Economic Work" (10 Jan.1945) in Quotations from Chairman Mao, Peking 1967, pp.187-188.
21) With the notable exception of minority areas, where population growth is tolerated, and even encouraged. Thus, the historical birth rate in 1974 in the Inner Mongolia Autonomous Region was 2.1% and in the Xinjiang Autonomous Region 3% per annum. Cf. Peking Review No.40, 12 Oct.1974.

They allowed China - if the reports from foreign visitors coming out of the country are correct - to reduce the demographic expansion rate by more than 50 % and eventually bring population growth under control.

The implementation of these policies was well under way when the First Five-Year Plan came to an end. They were expanded, popularized and intensified to such an extent that foreign observers with an ample background of experience in the Chinese rural milieu both before and after Liberation could report that during the last years of the Fourth Five-Year Plan (1971-1975), the raw birth rate in practically all the villages they visited had already fallen below 2 % (22), and for the most part much lower.

A great deal about the Chinese effort to limit demographic expansion and bring down the birth rate, particularly in the villages, has become known to the outside world from travellers' reports during recent years. As population policy is not strictly within the scope of this study, the present discussion will focus not on its details but limit itself to mentioning its results as attained by the mid-1970s.

A second lesson of the First Plan lay in the recognition that for her industrialization, China would have to rely on her own forces much more than anticipated and that if foreign capital contributions could still be expected - they were becoming more and more conditional - they would attain only less than decisive volume. Closely connected with this was the insight that her specific factor composition did not allow China to follow the Soviet approach to economic development with optimal results. To mention only two decisive differences: when Stalin launched the first Soviet Plan, the U.S.S.R. had abundant land and known raw material deposits, whereas China had very little of both, pending the outcome of country-wide prospecting campaigns. Secondly, the Soviet Union had a very favourable man/land ratio, while China's was unfavourable. Consequently, the U.S.S.R. could afford to make mistakes and pay for experiments with a certain amount of waste; China could not, particularly not in agriculture. The results of the First Plan period had made it clear that even without squeezing agriculture for surpluses, the rural economy would remain vulnerable for some time and expand only slowly; that the stage of socialist integration thus far attained did not yet generate the quantities of food and cash crops needed to pay for an even higher rhythm of industrialization; and that the productive land base was expanding only slowly, while enormous amounts of

---

22) R.Dumont, Chine: La Révolution Culturale, Paris 1976.

manpower remained idle or underemployed. This led to considerable debate about alternative ways of proceeding, ending with a victory for the bold innovators who claimed that China, by shifting emphasis in factor and sector utilization, could not only make up for her unfavourable resource endowment but even improve upon the Soviet method of building socialism.

Among the major results of these theoretical debates were the concepts of the People's Commune and the Great Leap Forward.

The commune concept grew out of the awareness that the advanced cooperatives were still too small and too poor to allow a quick transition to really modern farm management methods, especially if the burden of capital equipment was not to fall upon the State and its central investment fund. If the current rates and directions of surplus generation and utilization and of investment flow were to be maintained, the rural production units would have to become much more active, particularly by modernizing crop production through mechanization and by rural capital construction. A rural infrastructure would have to be created not by state investment, but mainly by the user communities themselves, the State entering only exceptionally in a supporting role. For this, larger, more rational units were necessary, more actively to mobilize local savings capital and to supplant the lacking financial resources by manpower.

The key of these theories was obviously manpower. In the same way as Nurkse but earlier, the Chinese had perceived that the unutilized working capacity of their manpower represented latent savings that could replace what China lacked most: capital. The Nanniwan project and other experiments in the Yanan period had convinced the leadership of the feasibility of such an approach, particularly if it was combined with two other features: an appeal to the innate inventiveness of the labouring masses to find ways and means of bypassing bottlenecks in equipment and technology (which went under the catchword "Walking on Two Legs", i.e., making use of native make-do formulas), and the conviction that if manpower was sufficiently concentrated, properly motivated and well led, hardly a problem would remain that could not be solved (an attitude which went under the name of "Self-Reliance"). Armed with these two strategic tools, so the innovators argued, China's rural labour force would be able to overcome the barriers of low productivity and lack of capital and technology, and could create the preconditions for greater surplus generation until industry in turn took over and relieved the toiling masses by providing them with mechanical implements. In this way China would eventually raise labour productivity and free labour reserves for transfer into more modern production sectors.

From this viewpoint the Great Leap Forward brought not only the well-known advances in quantitative output for whose ephemeral nature it was so roundly criticized and written off abroad, but also remarkable qualitative changes. China's revolutionary manpower policies are one of the lasting achievements of this experiment. Although a great deal was still sketchy, tentative and often over-zealous in the 1958-1960 period, the basic approach proved to be correct, while its practical applications could be refined and adapted to a great extent in later years. Fundamentally, the decision to abandon the Soviet model, at least in part, in favour of one more adapted to Chinese conditions, especially by greater use of existing labour reserves, is a positive achievement of the Great Leap that outweighs shortcomings in the first trials.

Moreover, at the beginning of the Second Five-Year Plan, China still counted on support by the U.S.S.R., which was committed to deliver not only farm machinery but plant equipment, that would allow China to build her own farm machinery, especially tractors. With this equipment, the rural collectives would quickly manage the transition to mechanized agriculture with its concomitant large increases in output and surpluses. But in order to use the forthcoming material rationally, even larger management units would have to be created.

Out of these two considerations grew the concept of the large-scale rural unit, combining on average seven advanced cooperatives into one new entity that would assume not only production but also administrative, social and cultural functions. It was meant to be the basic unit of socialist communal existence of the future.

This new "Commune" - so named in memory of the Paris Commune of 1871 - immediately became an essential ingredient of the almost simultaneously inaugurated Great Leap Forward. This drive set aside the original Second Plan and its targets, to a large extent de-activated central planning itself and replaced it by general instructions to over-fulfil the plan in three years instead of five or, generally, to "aim as high as possible". The rationale behind this seems to have been that growth rates in industry (the centrally administered modern production sector) could be maximized in two ways: by concentrating as much of the centrally available investment funds as possible on the expansion of further capacity, and by rechanneling the profits generated by this sector back into investment (although these funds took the detour through the fiscal accounts, it boiled down in fact to sectoral auto-financing). All this was designed to permit industry to reach as quickly as possible the stage of socialist accumulation and self-expanding reproduction from which industrialization could continue under its own momentum.

Agriculture, which had received only 8 % of all centrally allocated investment in the First Plan, was not intended to receive a greater share of central budgetary investment. However, the agricultural tax, which had been fixed in absolute terms, was allowed to decline relative to output (23). Nor were procurement prices considerably changed at first. Increased surplus accumulation by fiscal authorities was mainly obtained by increases in the sales tax on agricultural inputs and consumer goods, which averaged 40 % of total sales proceeds.

A second way of obtaining a greater contribution from agriculture was opened by the introduction of the "Three-Thirds" policy, under which the newly formed communes were to devote a third each of their cultivable land to food production, cash crops and forestry. Unfortunately, however, a misunderstanding thwarted the implementation of the policy. The government had intended it as a guideline for gradual adoption and echelonned diversification. The lower levels, however, mistook it for a stringent order for immediate action. This led in many places to its abrupt introduction into collectives which had barely recovered from the initial upheavals of their restructuring under the commune system. They neither were ready for it nor had the managerial experience to know what was feasible under local conditions, and especially when to renounce implementation in order to avoid damage.

Thirdly, the communes were assigned the task of developing small-scale industrial enterprises to shoulder the responsibility of supplying much of the agricultural inputs and consumer goods that should have been provided by the central industry sector, which was to be relieved of this burden in favour of a higher rate of auto-expansion. Finally, the communes were charged with rural capital construction, for which all surplus manpower was to be mobilized, especially in the slack season. In this way agriculture was to repeat what industry was meant to do: expand its basis by its own strength and without counting on budgetary help on a major scale. At the same time it was still expected to generate surpluses for the rest of the economy.

---

23) From 12% of gross output value in 1953 to about 3 to 5% in 1974.

This strategy counted heavily on the use of the labour force in the new communes. It was clear that regimentation could never ensure the villagers' free and wholehearted collaboration and therefore it was not even envisaged, notwithstanding misleading external interpretations. Instead, the leadership founded the new labour relations among the peasant population upon an extension of the already existing system of work and remuneration. The communes now offered the population a new and all-embracing social relationship. They promised to provide and guarantee the peasants a comprehensive livelihood, the elements of which can be summed up by the so-called "Five Guarantees" enshrined in China's constitutional legislation: food, shelter, clothing, health care, a minimum of education - and in addition, to the dead a decent burial - all on the basis of the Marxian principle of "To each according to his performance, from each according to his ability." In exchange, the villagers were to devote their working capacity to the commune, in practice 250 to 300 workdays a year for men, 220 to 250 for women. This concept fulfilled the first requirements of Marxian socialism: a just and equitable system of production relations, while on the village level it offered unheard-of security and stability to the mass of the former rural proletariat and small and medium peasants who had been accustomed for generations to eke out an existence of insecurity, deprivation and instability. The response therefore was predictably enthusiastic.

The system did not do away with all private activities. On the contrary, sideline activities of rural households, private plots, etc., were safeguarded, but - and this is the essential point - not for productive activity in the framework of the national or local economy but only for supplementary personal use. It was initially not envisaged to authorize the commercialization of the produce from private plots (although subsequently the authorities, acting pragmatically, relaxed their position on this point), which were to serve only to round out family consumption levels of such items as fruit, vegetables, rabbits, poultry, etc.

As is now known, the burden of the Great Leap proved too heavy and the rural sector caved in after two years of gigantic efforts. The 1960 harvest proved a near-disastrous failure. The reasons, insofar as they are relevant to employment policy, were the following:

- During 1952-59 China had benefited from a stretch of unusually favourable crop weather which had been mistaken for normal. By 1959 the meteorological trend reversed, and one weather calamity after another broke upon the country. Immediate relief work would have been necessary, especially in replanting lost seeds, draining flooded areas, water adduction in those hit by drought, etc. But the commune apparatus, then very rigid and not yet fully broken in, did not allow the necessary shifts of labour into such emergency tasks, and what shifts were possible came too slowly.

- The "Three Thirds" policy, understood by most commune leaders as an immediate call for change in the cultivation pattern rather than as a long-term goal, proved a premature step and therefore had unfortunate effects. Not only had the food crop area been tragically reduced but scarce inputs had been diverted away from food production when the latter would have needed increased help.

- The commune structure, with its premature emphasis upon the pre-eminence of its top tier and the formation of units large both with respect to area and to labour at the expense of its smaller components, the brigades (former cooperatives) and work teams, was too unwieldy for snap decision-making and spot adaptation. The large new peasant units were forced into passivity, while orders from above either came too late or were irrelevant to immediate local needs, or both.

- Above all, unbridled pursuance of afforestation, capital construction and small-scale industrialization, and continued insistence on them while crop work cried for more hands, had resulted in large-scale misallocations of manpower. Most communes reported gaping shortages of labour not only during the harvest season but almost throughout the whole crop year, while nearby hundreds of farmers were smelting steel, mining iron ore and coal, building small fertilizer plants, digging irrigation channels. This chronic and increasing shortage of manpower for crop work, due to over-zealous diversification, seems to bear a major share of responsibility in the dramatic failure of the villages to increase agricultural output further, or even maintain the previously attained level in the face of sudden adversities.

- At the same time, political relations with the Soviet Union worsened. The U.S.S.R. withdrew her experts and discontinued the supply of equipment for many of the industrial plants scheduled to go onstream during the Second Plan. With this the hopes for an early transition to agricultural mechanization collapsed.

Corrective manpower policies during the Consolidation Period

When the repercussions of the Great Leap Forward reached industry and caused widespread cutbacks in production and in some cases complete stoppage of plants and projects, the government lost little time in redeploying immobilized manpower. At first, unemployed urban workers were sent to the surrounding countryside in emergency operations to help out where agricultural collectives were in need of more labour. Subsequently, the planning authorities undertook more systematic assessments of what industrial labour force would still be needed under a consolidation policy and how much of it, especially from the city-wide and industry-wide so-called "labour pools" of semi-skilled and unskilled workers, would become redundant. The latter were forthwith sent back to their villages to reinforce the rural labour potential while freeing the cities from unemployed consumers. According to the Minister in charge of Planning, Bo Yibo (24), ten million workers and about ten million dependents were thus returned to their villages.

At the same time, the "Three Thirds" policy was called off for the time being, and afforestation, capital construction and rural industrialization schemes were severely curtailed. Only those projects were permitted to continue which showed economic viability and guaranteed possibilities of future technical or social usefulness. The rest were either cut back or switched to another, safer line of production, or scrapped outright. The additional labour force thus rendered redundant was also reassigned to field work.

With this emergency strategy focusing again on maximizing labour utilization and greater flexibility in labour deployment, the government was able to check tendencies, especially in disaster areas, to abandon villages and fields, as had happened too often in the past when large-scale catastrophes had struck down the crops, and to forestall aimless floating migration by uncounted thousands. It managed to fix the villagers in their economic environment and to encourage them to fight back, replant destroyed fields, replace lost crops with fast-growing alternative plantings, restore necessary infrastructural facilities such as burst dams, ruptured irrigation ducts, etc. Local responsibility for the prompt execution of these measures was entrusted to the party organs in the communes, which

---

24) In an interview with A.L.Strong, A.L.Strong's Letter from China, No.22, Peking 1964.

virtually took over command from the administrative committees. Where reliable cadres were lacking, army personnel were sent down, as well as experienced party personnel from the towns.

With the outlook for the winter of 1960/61 grim, policy instructions went out to put all available forces into food production, which was to be maintained and raised by all means and with no reference to earlier policy and planning decrees. Ancillary measures - which in some cases survive until the present day - established sharp controls and prohibitions of all unauthorized labour movements, introduced rationing (24a), and forbade all large-scale deployment of commune labour without the consent of the competent commune, brigade and team organs. Commune cadres were charged with finding appropriate ways of self-help and ensuring that crop work was always given top priority and that a wide safety margin was observed in the allocation of local manpower. The calamity had driven home the lesson that at the currently attained productivity levels, rural labour surpluses were conditional and should be so handled as never again to expose food production to critical shortages in labour inputs. The positive aspect, on the other hand, was that the commune structure had not only sustained the pressures of the crisis but had been instrumental in averting much worse an outcome.

From 1961 onward, Government and Party reformulated their development strategy in the light of the aborted Great Leap. It had become impossible to maintain the present priority order of economic construction, with emphasis upon heavy industry and a supporting role for agriculture, so long as food security for the whole nation was not attained and the commune system was so undeveloped that the agricultural sector could not assume self-sustenance in inputs and consumer goods supply. This was not only a matter of methodology of economic development but, as Chou En-lai explained in 1971, a recognition of political and strategic fundamentals. China had been

---

24a) Rationing of food grains and cooking oil was first introduced in 1955 in the cities as a measure to check rural migration. Arrivals from the villages would not only be unable to procure food but would soon be found out and could thus be sent back to the villages. Although this measure was not originally an outgrowth of the shortages, it became a useful tool for dealing with them in the aftermath of the Great Leap and has been retained, again as a measure to check undesirable labour movements, even though food shortages have been overcome long since.

forced to export foodstuffs to the U.S.S.R. throughout the Year of Calamity in order to pay for past industrial deliveries. To make up for these exports, she had begun to buy grain and feeds on the world market, with further disruptions in her supply system and industrial construction schedule as a consequence. It was therefore concluded that socialism could be built only when independence in essential supplies had been secured. The latter began for China with "self-sufficiency in agriculture, and here the first requisite is to have enough to eat" (25). Or, differently formulated, (26) "production had to come before procurement and secure living standards before accumulation". This was a viewpoint which Mao himself had expressed in 1956 in his essay on the "Ten Great Relationships". Consequently, the whole national development strategy, not only in narrow economic terms but in the wider sense of the striving for a new economic order, political independence and national self-determination, hinged upon the problem of ample self-sufficiency in food supplies and security of the nation's livelihood, without which all ambitious advances in surplus accumulation would remain in jeopardy.

This recognition led to a reversal of the "General Line on Economic Construction". From 1961 onward the new priorities read: "Agriculture the foundation, industry the leading sector. Take grain production as the key link and strive for all-round development." (26 a)

This resolution of the CCP Central Committee not only reversed the major sectoral priorities but also prescribed a new pattern for commune development. Cultivation of foodgrains, and in a wider sense all food production, now assumed absolute precedence over all other aspects of agricultural activity. Only to the extent that food production and food supply were assured - and that meant in the first place self-sufficiency in the villages themselves, and in the second place the generation of marketable surpluses covering the needs of the urban population - could the communes gradually devote more land and more labour to cash crop cultivation, reforestation and other activities. The former overambitious Three-Thirds policy had thus been reworked; far from having been jettisoned, it had been put into

---
25) Prime Minister Chou, quoted in P.Corrigan, "China: Socialist Construction as Thought Reform", in Journal of Contemporary Asia, Vol.4, no.3, 1974, p.285.
26) T.T. Mao, "On the Ten Great Relationships", Peking Review No.1, Jan.1964.
26a) Ta Kung Pao, Hong Kong, 1 Sept. 1962.

proportion and harmonized with the country's hierarchy of needs - and here, food overruled any other - and the communes' real possibilities. What was not possible for the moment was not ruled out for all time but postponed until the general upturn in output and productivity eventually made it feasible.

The commune structure, which had proved its usefulness, was maintained, but, since with the cessation of Soviet assistance the prospects for rapid mechanization had faded, the size of the average commune was drastically reduced. On average, each existing commune was divided into three smaller ones. Within them, much more responsibility for management and execution of production work was transferred downward to the teams and brigades, which received the right to reject all plans that would have resulted in taking away more than 5% of their labour force for commune projects and larger undertakings, if this appeared to endanger the implementation of their crop production plans.

A second most important decision was to relieve agriculture of responsibility for surplus generation for industrial development. On the contrary, industrial development was to be oriented in future to providing more aid to agriculture by such means as giving investment priority to tractor and fertilizer plants and other industries providing inputs to food production. Fiscally, not only were turnover and sales taxes in agriculture slashed, but massive farm price supports and increasingly high procurement prices improved the terms of trade in favour of agriculture. The agricultural tax was kept constant, thus leaving the benefit from increased output almost entirely to the producer collectives. On the whole, it was reported (27) that over the 1953 - 1971 period the State channeled 23% more funds back into the agricultural sector than it collected through the agricultural tax. This, however, seems to include such indirect support as State investment in industries supplying agricultural inputs.

The indispensability of mechanization was expressly upheld, but as a relatively distant goal. In the meantime, labour-intensive and traditional approaches to crop work would have to be used. Capital construction by massive uses of temporarily unemployed manpower, especially in the slack season, had to continue and even to be intensified. Priority was given to water conservation and to irrigation and drainage work, as these factors had been identified as keys to greater intensification of cultivation

---

27) Peking Review No.37, 16 Aug.1975, pp.23-25.

and to the introduction of multiple-cropping systems. The rural industrialization drive was to resume, but more cautiously, with a wider view to the actual possibilities of the newly-created manufacturing capacities and to needs of the parent bodies: provincial and xian economic planning bodies were instructed to pay primary attention to maintaining a suitable balance between manpower allocations to crop work and to other activities, and to ensure that the rhythm of transfer of labour from cultivation work to commune and central sector industries took full account of the needs of agriculture and of contingencies in case of emergencies.

As a further consequence, the rural collectives underwent another major restructuring, the last up to the present: The communes of 1958 had been huge units, especially by Chinese standards, with 3,000 to 15,000 ha and a labour potential of 5,000 to 25,000 families. Inner structure had been largely subordinated to considerations of economy of scale: the brigades and work teams had lost most of their planning and organizing prerogatives. The leadership now reversed its position. The new, subdivided communes of 1961/62 saw their size reduced to 800 to 5,000 ha and 1,000 to 8,000 households. Cultivation, work management and work-point accounting as far as farming was concerned, reverted to the teams and less often to the brigades. In other words, strictly for crop production the countryside returned to the predominance of the village, with effective unit sizes of 10 to 100 ha, tilled in common by 20 to 100 households. Only the non-cropping activities were transferred to or remained with the brigades and communes proper. This order was to be retained until mechanization would become a reality at the village level.

The new policies were largely finalized and promulgated by the 10th Plenum of the 7th Central Committee in July 1962. From then onward, however, two schools emerged among the Chinese leadership, whose views on long-term guidelines and methods of agricultural reconstruction clashed more and more frequently. There were those who maintained that the strategy of the Great Leap Forward had been basically correct; that China needed a development methodology of her own and that here were the beginnings of such a concept; that the Years of Calamity had only been a temporary setback and that China after Consolidation should return to more aggressive economic policies. The other school, among which were now some who had been the most ardent supporters of the Great Leap and its more radical innovations, had been severely frightened by the setbacks of 1960/62. Its adherents were now inclined to advocate not only a temporary shelving of some of the premature novelties they themselves had introduced with the Great Leap, but also a broad renunciation of all the reforms they felt were too foolhardy and boldly unorthodox to achieve secure results.

This latter fraction, although a minority, temporarily gained the upper hand and not only imposed a virtual halt to the transformation of the rural productive organization but pushed through measures which resulted in a far-reaching erosion of the commune system itself. This policy, under the euphemism of "Three Freedoms and One Guarantee" (Sanzi Yibao), hinged essentially on the extension of the villagers' private plots, greater emphasis upon private sideline activities, greater freedom for private marketing and village markets with freely negotiated prices for agricultural commodities, and a general relaxation of planning and production control on the commune level in favour of greater private initiative and attention to profitability. In short, it was a policy of slower expansion in favour of greater stability. The proponents of this line, however, did not confine themselves to these points. They sought to carry the retreat from the policies of socialist integration even further, as far as the re-establishment of private holdings and their extension to parity with the socialist sector; the re-institution of the household as the basic accounting unit; a limited reprivatization of land, production factors and cultivation; the reintroduction of hiring labour and lending money; full commune autonomy in price- and wage-fixing; the abolition of output quotas; the lowering of the accumulation rate and even the dissolution of the accumulation funds; the establishment of financial profitability as the main operational criterion; and the reauthorization of private trade in agricultural produce and producer goods. Although the parallel is certainly fortuitous, these proposals bore a curious resemblance to the similar and simultaneous Zveno proposals which Andreyev had thrown into the Soviet agricultural debate in 1961.

This proposed new switch in agricultural development policies was attacked as an immense danger because it aimed not only at abolishing almost the entire commune policy and a great deal of the previously achieved socialist integration, but at a surrender of all hope of a rapid modernization of China's agricultural sector, and of the transformation of the nation into a modern, economically potent power. It also implied the re-establishment of antagonistic, antisocialist, disruptive elements in the midst of the Chinese rural society for a long period, probably for good - in short, the end of China's socialist dream.

A sharp struggle flared up, which gradually moved from the purely socio-economic level to the political one and in which the majority, grouped around Mao Tse-tung, finally won the day and enforced the return to a course that for the most part readopted the sounder policies of the Great Leap, but in a more refined form and with more articulated, sophisticated methods of application.

A victory of the "revisionists" would indeed have spelled unmitigated disaster for China's rural order, as hindsight easily shows. Return to the household as basic productive unit and partial reprivatization not only would have cancelled out all the achievements of rationalization in field work and land use obtained so far, but also would have closed the door to future improvements in labour productivity. Mechanization would have become practically impossible. Capital accumulation and investment on the basis of the villages' own savings power would have become impossible. The villages would again have become dependent on governmental contribution for investment. Rational mobilization of unemployed or redundant labour for capital construction and infrastructural improvements would have been either greatly hampered or entirely prevented. China's agriculture would have sagged back to the level of an atomized, low-productivity family economy, with none of the advantages and all the socially disruptive features found in pre-revolutionary China and contemporary Southeast Asia: low investment rate, high consumption, insufficient capital formation, great social disparities, unemployment, internal and floating labour migration, speculative price movements, hoarding, graft, corruption - in short, China would have foregone the immense advantages she now has over all other agricultural economies of the Asian continent. She would have lost all the tremendous dynamism which has propelled her agriculture forward during the last fifteen years.

Labour policies especially would have been gravely affected, and, indeed, they were to some extent, before the "revisionists" were finally defeated. Progressive manpower utilization, as it had been elaborated during the first three years of the Second Plan, was largely cut back. Labour investment schemes continued but on a more limited scale, mainly for repair of existing and already initiated small-scale projects. Thus, damage wrought by the natural calamities of the crisis years was repaired, and small-scale soil improvement, land reclamation and irrigation work continued, but few large-scale projects were taken on. Afforestation work diminished in scope and area wherever it went beyond village plantations, protective plantings, and wind-rows and shelterbelts within the commune framework. The nascent small-scale and commune industries were severely trimmed back and confined to such enterprises for which there was either a direct and persistent need, guaranteed outlets, or assured profitability at the level currently attained. Many new investments were postponed or shelved indefinitely. A sizeable part of the village labour force, particularly in the slack season, returned to private occupations, hired themselves out, went into petty trading. It was therefore fortunate - and it is the immense merit of Mao and his followers - that agricultural policies were checked and gradually led back, after the humanly necessary period of relaxation and consolidation, to the original strategy of collective, all-round expansion as embodied in the communes.

Implementing these policies in their broad lines, China proceeded through the period of Consolidation (1961-65) and two more Five-Year Plans (1966-70 and 1971-75).

CHAPTER VI

Employment Policies

During the Third and Fourth Plan Periods

The key factors in the revised approach were the commune and its inner structure, the emphasis in whose main conception shifted from the economic to the social aspect. The commune is henceforth conceived less and less as primarily a unit of land and increasingly as one of labour and, more generally, of population. Agriculture, although the most important, is only one of its productive functions, which may include any others that are feasible and useful from the viewpoints of internal well-being and of the State's overall development plans. Internally, the commune's divisions of labour ideally run along the following lines:

- the work team, in most cases the basic accounting and organizational unit (28), is responsible for basic production, i. e., work in the fields and some small-scale poultry- and pig-raising;
- the production brigade organizes secondary activities such as animal husbandry, large-scale poultry- and pig-raising, fish breeding, fruit-growing, small-scale irrigation, water conservation, soil improvement and domestic land reclamation work, small-scale forestry such as for shelterbelts and fuel wood plantations, small-scale industries for processing farm products and sideline production, and small maintenance and repair shops;
- the commune looks after large-scale irrigation and soil conservation, tractor and machine stations, power generation and all heavier commune industry. It manages the experimental and demonstration farms and stations, larger animal-husbandry stations, forest farms, etc., which have been created over time, larger-scale land reclamation, afforestation and other capital construction projects undertaken either alone or in collaboration with other communes.

---

28) According to the new Constitution of the PRC of January 1975, the <u>work team</u> is "the basic accounting unit", i. e., other arrangements are exceptions.

This, of course, is only a schematic breakdown and there are many exceptions. The borderline between the various tiers of occupational jurisdiction are fluid and largely a product of empirical development. On each level, the management of the production collective is relatively autonomous in its decisions on manpower deployment and only indirectly bound by obligations arising from plan targets and annual delivery agreements with the xian authorities. It is for the communes to see by what methods of labour utilization they fulfill their obligations. Only if for instance some of the broad national guidelines on manpower utilization are violated, or if overall employment persistently remains below what could be called full employment at the village level, do xian authorities step in. Cases such as those were reported during the Years of Consolidation, when over-cautious commune committees allowed too much slackening of labour discipline and labour intensity.

Under the current overall policy, a great deal of manpower development has taken place since the early 1960s. A prominent place has been taken by the promotion of female labour. Thanks to persistent prodding from the State, most communes now attain participation rates of well over 75% of all adult women (29). (On the other hand, by 1970 only 20 to 30% of all skilled rural medical personnel were said to be women (30), a figure that appears to be very low.)

A second major improvement lies in the flexible use of retired people. The official retirement age is 55 for men and 50 for women, but most people past retirement age who still desire an occupation are still largely employed, on a time or hourly basis, at jobs commensurate with their physical and mental strength. The collective thus continues to benefit from the experience of its veterans, while the latter not only have the feeling of still being active and contributing to the common welfare, but also still have the opportunity of earning work-points.

Inversely, child labour, from which the ancient landlord estates derived a large part of their revenue, has been completely abolished. Pupils of the older age groups are gradually introduced to productive labour by work on off-days and short stints during school vacations or during

---

29) Dumont, op.cit., p.82, reports a typical case from Chengtiefang Brigade, Xianhua Xian, Hebei, where in 1974 42.5% of all labour inputs were furnished by women.
30) A.P. Khan, Distribution of Income in Rural China, ILO, Geneva 1976, p.53.

harvest time. But this, especially in the beginning, is more in the nature of training than of real production labour. Most adolescents, even in rural areas, now obtain at least five or six years of school education, plus one or several training courses in professional skills. When they enter the active work force, they are no longer unqualified but have at least basic notions about the most common jobs required in their community. Later on, a far-flung adult evening and spare-time educational system imparts further skills and specializations, so that the commune labour force steadily improves the range and quality of its training.

Within such broad policy guidelines on employment, training and qualification, the commune authorities bear full responsibility for the concrete use of their collectives' labour force.

Employment in agriculture

Employment in farming itself has been greatly affected by the rationalization and intensification measures taken since 1958, such as the creation of much larger fields, often of one, two, even ten and more hectares, mostly only after labour-consuming land levelling and terracing. Further improved cultivation measures prescribed in the Eight-Character Charter, such as deep ploughing, re-planting and transplanting, not only of rice but increasingly also of wheat, further increased labour requirements, as did the use of chemical fertilizers in several applications per crop season; the spreading of natural fertilizing matter, often carried by shoulder pole, in order to increase the humus layer; the adoption of dense-planting techniques; the tending of growing plants in dense-planted fields so that all could receive sun, air and humidity; and finally harvesting. These innovations were only a precondition for the promotion of former single-crop areas to multi-cropping. This latter system in turn required the adduction of much more water, at first and for many years obtained through hand pumps, treadmills, the installation of gravity channels and pipelines, even the hauling of water in barrels, until mechanized pump-wells could be installed. It is therefore plausible that already during the Great Leap Forward, labour inputs in the various cultivation categories exceeded the pre-war averages by several times (although the pre-war statistics include only cultivation in the narrow sense of the term, while the 1958 figures seem to comprise also such indirect inputs as providing irrigation, transporting and spreading compost and manure, carrying out plant protection and pest eradication measures, etc.).

Table 4

Average labour inputs in crop cultivation 1930 and 1958

(in man/days per crop-mou)

Crop category	1930	1958
Rice	13.66	35
Wheat	4.33	13.4
Maize	3.88	16.9
Cotton	8.80	18.1

Source:
1930: J.L. Buck, Land Utilization in China, Chicago 1937, p.156. Calculated on the basis of observations in five eastern provinces.
1958: Renmin Ribao, Peking, 11 Nov. 1958.

Since 1958, multiple-cropping alone surely must have driven labour requirements up considerably further. This assumption is bolstered by the rise in the multiple-cropping index from 145 (1959) to 185 (1972) [31]. More recent reports speak of provincial cropping indexes of 200 and 250 [32]. Statements in the Chinese press declare that by 1974 triple-cropping had become the predominant cultivation pattern south of the Yangtze [33], etc. Individual communes reported that by 1974 their annual labour inputs had reached three times and more the number of man-days reported for 1957. If this is compared with what happened in other countries that still recently had passed through the developing stage, this is nothing extraordinary. In Japan for instance, the average labour input per rice crop exceeded 160 man-days/ha in

---

[31] H.V. Henle, Report on China's Agriculture, FAO, Rome 1974, p.91.
[32] Hsinhua, Peking, 9 Oct.1975.
[33] Peking Review No.46, 14 Nov.1975, p.15.

1954, excluding the voluminous preparatory work obviously included in the Chinese accounts. (By 1969 the figure had fallen to 109, a reduction that can be explained only by the intensive mechanization that took place in the meantime.)

Another important factor contributing to increases in overall requirements for commune manpower must be the horizontal extension of cultivation, i. e., that of the arable land area, which between 1949 and 1958 increased by 16.6 million hectares; it was said to have increased again by 12.2 million hectares between 1958 and 1972, for an average of nearly 800,000 ha a year. This latter figure corresponds roughly to the semi-official annual increase figures. Thus, according to the then Vice-Premier Hua Guofeng (34), the figure reached 1.6 million hectares/year during the Fourth Plan. Similar effects must have been produced by the annual average expansion of terrace fields by 670,000 ha during the Fourth Plan period alone; the introduction of cold- and drought-resistant varieties, e. g., in Xinjiang and Tibet, where wheat is now grown at altitudes of up to 4,000 m and chingko barley at over 4,000 m; or the improvement of red lateritic soils in South China (covering 30 to 40% of the area south of the Yangtze), which brought nearly seven million hectares from near-zero productivity to near-average yields by 1975.

One aspect deserving special attention is the large number of drives for small but steady improvements in factor quality and hence productivity. For example in hilly areas Chinese extension services taught the farmers the "raised field" system (taitian), under which each plot is surrounded by irrigation ditches, the earth dug out being used to raise the surface of the plots. Over the years, the field level rises and increasing amounts of topsoil otherwise washed away are recovered. A next step, terracing, further facilitates retention of water and topsoil, drainage of excess water, and conservation of soil nutrients, and reduces silt losses by 85 to 95% and water losses by 90% and more. Work on such small-scale soil improvement measures is estimated at 20 to 30 man-days/hectare, levelling and raising field levels may require 75 to 150 man-days/hectares per year, and other soil improvement measures (such as freeing the plots from stones, etc., deep ploughing, and adding clay, mull or other substances to improve soil quality) between 20 and 100 man-days/hectare/year. Wells with stone revetment, increasingly

---

34) Peking Review No.44, 31 Oct.1975.

recommended and common, may take 200 to 1,000 man/days or even more to sink (35).

All this explains why individual communes reported that their manpower utilization has increased by leaps and bounds during the last years. For example, Liuji, a commune in Hubei, reported that the number of man-days invested in grain-crop cultivation, tending, pruning and harvesting its orchards and cotton fields doubled in three years after the effects of irrigation, drainage and soil improvement work and HYV (35 a) use, undertaken during the Third Plan period (1966-70), began to be felt. Liuji also reported that in spite of some semi-mechanization and mechanization, manpower requirements were further expected to rise steeply. Future target fulfilment would essentially depend on proportional increases in labour productivity (36).

The least that can be said is that the effects on employment, labour productivity, output, etc., of cultivation reform as prescribed in the Eight-Character Charter are far-reaching and interrelated, and that they are probably still far from having reached the limits of feasibility. On balance it is probably safe to assume that, thus far, increases in labour requirements for farming have been greater than labour savings from the rationalization of crop work and from other rationalizations made possible by the improved organizational structure of the communes.

Below are given a few further examples of labour requirements recently observed (37):

---

35) Ministry of Irrigation and Water Control, Handbook on Erosion Control (Shuitu Baochi), Peking 1973.
35a) HYV = high yielding variety, of grains or other food, feed or cash crops. The Chinese initially preferred the term "improved seeds". Later on, this latter term was retained for those seeds that had been objects of a first genetic improvement and whose yields, although already much higher than ordinary ones, were still not yet comparable to the very considerable yield increments of the second generation.
36) Hsinhua, Peking, 24 .Sept.1975.
37) Dumont, op. cit., pp.47-127, and Ministry of Irrigation and Water Control, Handbook on Erosion Control, Peking 1973, pp.207-208.

Paddy rice cultivation (Guangdong)	315 Man-days/ha crop
Fertilizer application by hand (Guangdong)	20 man-days/ha
Sugar cane (planting to harvest)	900 man-days/ha (525 in 1955 and 450 in 1964)
Deep-ploughing (Henan) (0.7m deep)	900-1200 man-days/ha
Irrigation (digging of canals and ditches)	100 man-days/ha
Terracing (light soil, Guangdong)	200 man-days/ha
Land reclamation (Henan, mountainous terrain)	6000-7500 man-days/ha
Levelling	120-150 man-days/ha
Soil improvement	75-100 man-days/ha
Digging of irrigation ditches	45-100 man-days/ha benefitted
Digging of large wells	200-1000 man-days
Aquaculture (carp-breeding, pond conservation, three hauls per year)	1500 man-days/ha
Reforestation (hilly area, upper Guangdong)	270 man-days/ha
River bed reclamation	5000-15000 man-days/ha

Summing up the evolution of employment in field work, it is certainly safe to say that the implementation of the Eight-Character Charter, and the qualitative improvements of agricultural practices it brought with it, generated a huge increase in labour requirements. These requirements had and have to be met at the lowest organizational level, that of the work teams and production brigades, where manpower reserves had been gradually sponged up until steps towards rationalization had to be taken. As the implementation of the Eight-Character Charter continues - in fact, it is doubtful that one will ever be able to speak of full implementation since progress in agricultural techniques is steady and the Chinese intend to adopt whatever technical advances they find useful in their struggle for more output and higher productivity - the pressure towards more rational use of all available rural manpower will certainly grow. Unless the now competing alternative demands of rural industries, infrastructural capital construction, etc., are artificially curbed, they will force the intra-communal production units into taking increasing action to raise labour productivity. This already seems to be the case in advanced collectives; for the others it is due in the near future, probably during the current Fifth Plan.

Small-scale rural industries

The economic debate at the end of the First Five-Year Plan gave birth to the basic ideas behind this approach to overcoming China's lack of capital by mobilizing manpower resources and local savings. Experience since the Yanan days had suggested that the creation of a widely-scattered light industry was indeed feasible and might be well adapted to the prevailing rural conditions. Its emergence would help to relieve the load on the central sector and yet lead to increased accumulation without emburdening agriculture. Earlier experiments had shown that the capital/output ratio would be much lower than in State industry. A much faster amortization of investments, much lower capital intensity, a zero opportunity cost of labour in the rural setting outside the peak crop season, significant reductions in transport bottlenecks, avoidance of heavy social costs arising from urban industrialization, and development of backward areas would be other advantages. Such a rural industry would open visible outlets for the accumulated savings of the village population, allow the use of locally mastered technology and develop a dynamic and complementary relationship between agriculture and light industry in a localized framework. From the viewpoint of employment, it mopped up a great deal of rural manpower and diminished the attraction of migration to urban areas.

The exceptionally low capital intensity and rapid returns on investment were seen as two major advantages. An early appraisal (38) gave the following figures:

Table 5

Large-scale and small-scale industry, comparison

	Sector	
	State Industry	Local Industry
Average fixed capital per worker employed	8000 ¥	790 ¥
Output per 1000 ¥ of fixed capital	990 ¥	1314.0 ¥
Total value of annual production per worker	7920 ¥	1059.4 ¥

Undoubtedly, these were still preliminary figures, but no later ones have been published.

Once it had been decided to create a widespread network of small-scale rural industries, the government established a number of principles and priorities. Concentration was to be focused upon:

1. agro-industries, including the processing of agricultural produce as well as the production of agricultural inputs such as tools, fertilizers, etc.

---

38) Y.Y. Fan, "Brief Discussion on Profit/Capital Ratios and the Principle of Rapid Construction", in Jihua Jingji no.8, Peking 1958, quoted in S.Ishikawa, "A Note on the Choice of Technology in China", in Journal of Development Studies, London, October 1972, Vol.9, no.1, p.161 et seq.

2. extractive industries and utilities (mining, smelting, power generation);
3. basic consumer goods (clothes, household goods, etc.);
4. at a subsequent stage, sub-contracting and supply of components to the State-sector industries.

In fulfilling these tasks, the commune industry was to build capital for the direct or indirect use of the communes, to train large numbers of skilled and semi-skilled technical workers on whom the State industry could later draw, to contribute to local self-sufficiency, and to help eliminate differences in living standards between rural and urban communities.

After a first burst of expansion during the Great Leap, the commune sector was trimmed back considerably during the Consolidation Period in order to ensure that further investments by communes went only into technically sound and economically useful ventures. A second vigorous expansion began with the Third Plan and has continued since that time. Already in 1964, the commune sector was said to comprise

over	20,000	small plants manufacturing tools and agro-machinery,
	136	major farm machinery factories
	19,000	chemical plants (nearly 6,000 of which were producing fertilizer, pesticides, etc.)
over	20,000	construction material plants,
	16,000	saw-mills,
	6,100	mines,
over	100,000	handicrafts cooperatives, etc., undoubtedly most of them of small to miniscule size but capable of growing over the time.

In 1972, commune industries accounted for the following percentages of total national output:

food processing	59%
chemicals and fertilizers	54%
metal working	26%
agricultural implements	46%
building materials	72%
household goods	38% (39).
steel production	11%

During the same year, in many communes the contribution of the industrial enterprises to the total commune budget

---

39) Hsinhua, Supplement No.23, Peking, 31 Dec.1973.

exceeded 50%. In 1973 the global net value of the commune industry output was 34.6 billion ¥ (40) and for 1974 it amounted to 14 % of the country's total industrial output (41).

A field of application of the small-scale industry drive that is of particular importance to agriculture is the rural fertilizer industry. According to rough estimates by Buck and T. H. Shen, not more than 40% of China's farmland received any fertilization at all before 1949. As it was clear that yields could not be raised decisively without adequate applications of fertilizer, the government gave high priority to the creation of a national fertilizer industry, and the first large-scale plants went up during the First Plan. But it was already apparent that, if China's agriculture had to rely on the national industry sector only, it would take many years before sufficient supplies were available. Consequently, during the Great Leap, the central planners ordered that some of the newly-created village steel smelters be converted into fertilizer plants (42).

One type then emerging was that of a small-scale plant to exploit the sizeable deposits of potassium salts that had been discovered in several provinces. Anhui, a province which was particularly active in this field, had by 1970 created thirteen such plants, with a total capacity of 59,000 tons. Other types of small fertilizer factories were developed at about the same time and several machine-tool plants in the State sector were directed to specialize in the serial production of plant equipment that the communes and *xian* could buy from their own accumulation funds and then assemble with only a few technicians as advisers. A major prototype of this early stage was a liquid ammonia plant of 800 tons annual capacity, that required only 200 tons of steel, could be set up by eight technicians, and cost 900,000 ¥ to the communes. A second, slightly more sophisticated type, with an installed capacity of 3,000 tons of ammonia and ammonium bicarbonate per year, cost 3.5 million ¥ and could be assembled and brought onstream

---

40) *China Today*, Peking, 18 Oct.1974.
41) C.Q. Chang, "On Exercising All-round Dictatorship over the Bourgeoisie", *Peking Review* No.14, April 1975, p.7.
42) It has not been generally realized abroad that the steel smelters were meant to be much more than the beginning of a metallurgical industry, but the basis for any industrialization in the rural setting in general. But instead of going directly into specialization and diversification, the Chinese started with basics, be it in technology, choice of products, or type of activity.

within six months; it was designed in such a way that capacity could subsequently be expanded to 8,000 tons. Most of these early plants have expanded considerably since the early 1960s and have added other production lines. Newer ones appear technically much more advanced.

This small-scale fertilizer industry grew by leaps and bounds: in 1971, in the decentralized sector, there were over 500 medium and small plants (with an annual capacity of 3,000 to 50,000 tons each) and about 7,000 very small plants within the communes. In addition, about 63,000 small workshops, many of them only seasonal and often with an output of only a few dozen tons, were said to be run by brigades. This local industry furnished about 60% of the national chemical fertilizer supply during the Fourth Five-Year Plan and in 1975 accounted for 15 to 16 million tons of industrial product (43). While the output was at first of low quality - 1% or less nutrient content - the local plants worked very hard to raise their quality standards and in the early 1970s were said by and large to have attained very satisfactory nutrient levels (i.e. 16-20% in the case of nitrogen products). Their contribution allowed Chinese agriculture to raise average annual consumption of chemical fertilizer to more than 150 kg/ha (industrial product). Some countries in Hunan and other southern provinces reported much more, 600 kg/ha and beyond, i.e. input levels approaching those reached by Japanese farmers in the 1960s. The sector is growing vigorously and, according to Chinese sources (44), its growth rate since 1960 has never been lower than 10%; often it has been much higher, reaching 15-16 % per year in 1975 and 1976. (45)

A good example of the development of such a small-scale fertilizer plant is the Dali Fertilizer Factory in Nanhai Xian, Guangdong, about 40 km west of Guangzhou (Canton). Started in 1952 as a small match factory, it closed down again until the plant was revived in 1959 as a sulphur-processing workshop producing sulphuric acid. During the later stage of the Great Leap, more production facilities were added by the commune, and from 1961 onward Dali produced 3,000 tons of synthetic ammonia and 800 tons of nitrogen annually. The number of workers rose from 210 in 1959 to 564 in 1964. In 1965, capacity was

---

43) Twenty-four per cent in 1973, cf. Hsinhua, Peking, 15 Jan. 1975.
44) Hsinhua, Peking, 13 Jan.1975.
45) At the end of the Fourth Plan, small-scale industry, which had grown by about 700 new plants in the xian and commune sectors between 1971 and 1975, contributed 69% of China's total fertilizer supply (Hsinhua, Peking, 24.Feb.1976).

again enlarged and the number of workers rose to 975. In the same year, ownership was transferred from Dali commune to Nanhai Xian, which compensated Dali for its investments. Products from the plant now go to all communes in Nanhai.

Technologically, the plant is a typical product of the Great Leap, most of its equipment having been manufactured in the commune's own workshop from blueprints furnished by larger, state-owned enterprises. Much of the remainder is scrap material from more modern plants of the state sector, salvaged by Dali's workers and reconditioned. Some production methods are therefore relatively modern and some still backward. Coal is supplied from commune mines in the <u>xian</u>, at a distance of 4 to 23 km. In 1972, according to its managers, the plant still had many problems, and was two years behind the plan targets. Sulphuric acid production still caused a great deal of pollution. Waste gases, liquids and solids were not yet being fully recycled or used as sources of further production. In 1972, output was

    4,350 tons of synthetic ammonia,
  30,000 tons of phosphate fertilizer,
  12,000 tons of sulphuric acid,
      90 tons of insecticides,
   2,000 tons of carbon dioxide base,
   2,500 tons of ammonium sulphate.

Other by-products were 2,000 tons of recovered iron and 160 tons of cement.

The total investment cost in the two stages since 1959 amounted to 6.1 million Y. The plant paid 6% of its gross revenue in industrial tax, and remittances to the <u>xian</u>'s accumulation fund were 18%.

To rationalize the further development of small-scale industry, the government laid down a number of further corrective guidelines: when such production factors as manpower are locally in short supply, first priority is to be given to agriculture and second to the State industry: the commune industry is not to compete for resources with either. Commune ownership patterns are to be observed; units must not use subordinate units' assets without the latters' consent and without compensation. Within communes, a rational division of labour should be observed, leaving bigger production projects - mainly manufacturing - for the communes and reserving smaller, technologically less sophisticated projects and most repair and maintenance functions to the brigades. Similarly, activities more closely related to agriculture, such as food processing, would be better carried out at the level closest to production; thus, food preservation, canning and pickling should be done at the brigade level, etc. The major part of the profits should be used not for consumption but for reinvestment, preferably in agriculture. Moreover, rural industry should not become a substitute for agricultural activities. (46) All this was intended to curb local pressures for all-out industrialization that might once more, as in the Great Leap, endanger agricultural production. On the other hand, it is true that some enterprises made exceptional progress and clearly broke through the initial framework of commune property and management. In such cases, the xian, the prefecture or sometimes even the provincial authorities took over, compensating the commune for its investment. It appears that many industrial enterprises managed today by xian, diqu or provinces, began as particularly successful commune plants.

From the viewpoint of employment, the commune industry sector was from its origins divided between year-round and seasonal operations. If brigades were to concentrate on maintenance and repair shops and on small-scale handicraft production, such as processing of cash crops, it was in order to keep employment flexible and allow enterprises to close down at harvest time, when rice was to be transplanted, and at other peak labour requirement phases of the crop year. Even today, most brigade enterprises appear to close down periodically in order to release workers for work in the fields.

The commune enterprises, however, usually function throughout the year, and by and large their labour force is today predominantly an industrial one with some degree of specialization, but even this does not preclude them from interrupting production in times of exceptional need in compliance with the governmental instruction that first priority must go to agriculture. By the end of 1975, Hsinhua reported, they had formed more than ten million specialized and technically skilled industrial workers, on whom the State industry sector could fall back when in need of qualified labour (47). Vice-Premier Zhang Chunqiao (48) reports that in 1974 commune industries employed 36% of all industrial labour.

What such an approach to industrial production can accomplish may be illustrated by two examples: early during the Fourth Plan, the industrial authorities of the Shanghai Municipal Region decided that the productivity of

---

46) Renmin Ribao, Peking, 14 Feb.1973.
47) Hsinhua, Peking, 30 Dec.1975.
48) Op. cit., p.8.

many of the city's slowly aging industries could be raised if their 1,000-odd boilers could be remodeled and/or refitted. For this, skilled manpower not only from the enterprises themselves but also from the surrounding communes and their factories were mobilized, and 200,000 welders and blacksmiths completed the entire job in 80 days (49).

In Yantai in northern Shandong, again, a small-scale steel complex based on local coal and iron ore was started in 1958. Manufacturing went so well that a small plant developed which by 1967 had outgrown the capacities of the original participating communes and was taken over by the diqu authorities. 75% of the labour force were former peasants and landless labourers trained on the job, and only 25% were local people who had been sent to Peking and Hangzhou for training. Capital investment from the local bodies had amounted to 75%, and the State had contributed about one fourth in a later phase only. Investment had been kept low by having the workers build their own halls and shacks, their own furnace and processing lines. 131 individual machines had been manufactured in the plant itself from blueprints provided by other enterprises which had assumed sponsorship of the Yantai complex. 77 machines were derived from discarded equipment from more modern State-sector plants, refitted and reassembled. Only 18 new machines had been provided by the State. Thus the total investment requirements had amounted to less than three million Yuan, of which 800,000 Yuan for a blast furnace, 500,000 Yuan the following year for a steel plant, and finally 1.4 million Yuan for parts of a rolling mill. In 1974, this plant produced 20,000 tons of raw steel and 17,000 tons of rolled steel, stainless steel and low alloys. 60% of this production was consumed by related farm machinery plants, which in 1974 manufactured 7,000 small caterpillar tractors, 33,000 diesel engines and 55,000 farm machines, pumps and other implements (50).

The Yantai example illustrates the pattern now followed by most enterprises of the small-scale and commune sector: starting usually either with artisan production or repair and maintenance, they remain at this level until a core of experienced, technically skilled workers has been formed and supply and delivery patterns are well established. They then acquire discarded machinery from some larger enterprise, selected operators receive in-plant training from donors in the State sector, and manufacturing of other equipment begins in the plant's

---

49) New China's First Quarter Century, Peking 1975, p.130 et seq.
50) Hsinhua, Peking, 3 Oct.1975.

own workshops. At first, production activities are at a very low output level. Prototypes are passed on to parental communes for experimentation. Only when everything, from the type and model of the future product to the production methods used, have been tested and run in, does the enterprise go fully onstream. Expansion and rationalization follow as more experience is gained and demand for its output increases. The paternal commune, the xian and if necessary, the State stand by with capital, technical advice and help in marketing. Even then the enterprise may continue for extended periods to import a large part of its components from outside manufacturers. The Xiyang tractor factory, for instance, after three years of successful production of a well-designed caterpillar tractor, in 1975 was still receiving from other producers more than 30% of its components, among them engines, which came from the Taiyuan Motor Works 160 km away.

Summing up the experience of the commune industries, it can be said that they proved better than more ill-conceived short-cuts to industrialization or unproductive employment programmes. Technologically, even if almost all plants started on what seemed a hopelessly primitive level, they showed that small-scale rural industry does not necessarily remain backward, and is capable of surmounting obstacles to higher technolgical levels almost completely under its own momentum. Economically, even if the early comparisons of capital requirements and output per unit of invested capital and worker may have been premature and over-optimistic, the Chinese experiment showed conclusively that manpower can replace financial resources to a surprising extent, that small-scale industries can function productively and improve their productivity, and that surplus generation is possible through them. From a development point of view, they demonstrated that in a general scarcity situation they can efficiently and quickly overcome bottlenecks and provide both agricultural inputs and consumer goods that otherwise, through the application of orthodox managerial and technological approaches, would have been impossible to procure, not only at permissible economic cost levels but under any material conditions, given the quasi-blockade under which China was forced to labour. From the standpoint of employment, the Chinese showed that even when there were great periodic fluctuations of manpower requirements in agriculture, the commune industry could sponge up a good deal of seasonal unemployment without sacrificing flexibility, thus preserving available a reserve labour force for periods of high needs and keeping labour mobility down. Excess development of capacity, capable of draining manpower from agricultural work, has been checked administratively, while subsidiarily the transfer of marginal labour to the urban sector always remains possible in case of need. Thus, two constraints have been imposed upon its further growth which may provide forceful incentives towards greater labour productivity. First, the prohibition to draw unrestrictedly upon farm labour acts as a push factor. Commune industry must stay within the limits of tolerance of farm labour supply imposed by crop productivity levels, which the commune industry can help to raise by making significant contributions. Second, the prospect of steadily losing some manpower to the central sector acts as a pull factor. In the past, such considerations may have been merely theoretical, as surplus manpower seems to have been readily available, but according to statements made at the Tachai Conference on Agriculture in September 1975, the point seems to have been reached where a permanent manpower pinch (in contrast to seasonal ones that seem to have been gradually removed by more appropriate balancing) is in sight in many rural areas.

A first question that may arise, as an apparent paradox, in the future is what will happen if agriculture, in the course of the Fifth Plan, runs into large-scale and more lasting labour shortages that cannot be removed by intraregional emergency shifts of local manpower surpluses, etc., and if attempts to raise labour productivity in crop work do not keep pace with requirements. Will commune industries then have to accept cutbacks? On the one hand, past government instructions clearly spell out the primacy of crop work and food production. On the other, permanent curbs on commune industry would hardly be acceptable in view of the importance the latter has gained in supplying agriculture with necessary production requisites. All this indicates that improvement of labour productivity may become, and perhaps soon, an absolute imperative for China's rural economy.

An altogether different aspect is capital accumulation. After some uncertainty, the Chinese perceived that commune industry was one device by means of which capital accumulation in the rural sector could be greatly activated. It could be brought to such a point that, without resorting to old and relatively crude devices such as the high sales-tax rates of the 1950s, it could finance a large part of the communes' own global investment requirements. Moreover, through taxes and sales of the State trading organizations, it could make a notable contribution to the government's own revenue. Curiously enough, this aspect has been minimized by Chinese official sources, who thus far have always insisted that after the 1962 change in the General

Line, of attributing first priority to agriculture, the State's investment in agriculture has been much greater than agriculture's remittances to the central fiscal funds. The scant figures made public always take an overview of the entire period from Liberation to the end of the Fourth Plan. It would be very interesting to see breakdowns by Plan periods, for they might show that a reversal is at hand, if indeed it has not taken place already.

Micro-economic information reaching the outside world strongly supports this hypothesis: reports from the Tachai Conference in September/October 1975 spoke of an exemplary ratio of accumulation to consumption in the model brigade itself and in all Xiyang County. Apparently, in 1973, the accumulation rate there had been 24%, while private consumption had taken 43% of total (net ?) revenue. Elsewhere, it was reported, the predominant accumulation rate had been around 10%, the implication being that there were still a number, perhaps even a high one, of production collectives whose accumulation rates had not yet reached this level and in which greater efforts had become desireable. (51)

The Chinese interest in high accumulation rates in rural collectives is only too understandable. A high accumulation in the communes renders the latter more capable of assuming larger investment burdens, thus lightening the State budget. More investment in the communes and their manufacturing capacity increases supply, hence better conditions for decentralized provision of production requisites and consumer goods. Moreover, the treasury benefits from the generation of more fiscal income in the form of the industrial tax remittances from the communes' manufacturing enterprises and of sales tax remittances generated by the marketing of the produce, agricultural as well as industrial.

Mass labour schemes for capital construction

The third, but by no means the least important, prong in the Chinese rural manpower strategy is the utilization of manpower in massive concentrations to build agricultural infrastructure and to provide the rural milieu with the physical equipment of a modern economy at the lowest

---

51) Hsinhua, Peking, 24 Sept.1975.

possible cost to the State budget (52). From their own experience in the years of struggle, the Chinese leaders knew that this was an area where underdevelopment made itself felt in the most typical, direct way. For it was axiomatic that developed countries were developed because they had what the underdeveloped lacked: the widely differentiated network of infrastructural facilities that constituted an indispensable precondition to socio-economic take-off. The Chinese therefore critically observed how other underdeveloped nations refrained from making any but the absolutely necessary investments in infrastructure as the latter are enormously money-consuming, slow in financial amortization, if amortizable at all, and, if created in technologically orthodox ways, often attainable only with foreign expert assistance. To the Chinese, on the contrary, the creation of a dense and capable infrastructural network appeared an essential ingredient to their progress to modernity, that had to rank at least equally in importance with such quick-maturing and highly profitable investments as in light industry (53). One crucial question was how to finance it in such a way that other investment programmes would not be dangerously retarded. Here the Chinese seem to have opted for two original principles:

- Not the State but the local users are principally responsible for the creation of rural infrastructure. It is for them to raise the necessary investment, the State intervening only by subsidy and on objects clearly beyond the reach of individual communities; hence relative emphasis must be placed on small and local objectives in preference to large-scale and nation-wide ones;
- Whenever monetary and fiscal capital can be replaced by manpower, if necessary in combination with local savings, this approach takes preference, so that funds can be saved for objectives for which manpower, non-monetized savings, etc., cannot replace financial capital.

(The Chinese benefit here from the fact that their collective ownership and collective management system in the villages is better suited to the tasks and problems

---

52) A Chinese term, characteristically understated, for this important aspect of the Communist development strategy is "Farmland and water conservation capital construction" (nongtian shuili jiben jianshe).
53) C. Ullerich, "China's GNP Revisited", Journal of Contemporary Asia, 1973, Vol.3, No.1, p.48 et seq.

of accelerated accumulation and manpower utilization. For it soon became obvious that their form of the collective system had most of the instruments and facilities needed to make maximal use of labour-intensive projects and to give strong incentives to their use as a substitute for financial and technical means. Since the commune and its leadership have a statutory obligation to provide food, income and employment to all members, the collective organs are under strong pressure to put all members to work, even at the lowest productive level, provided only that this work contributes to collective output and income. Contrary to what happens in private enterprise, the commune organs cannot lay off or discharge members when excessive labour use leads to declining revenues and marginal profits. They are obliged to carry their labour force for the better or the worse, as a constant factor in all their calculations. Therefore, as long as increments in labour utilization lead to any positive productivity, be it only the smallest addition to the aggregate product, commune committees have the strongest interest in using additional labour, whereas private management would not. Thus the collective system not only tends, but actually is compelled, to use more labour than any system of private enterprise and ownership, and also more than the Soviet kolkhoz system, in which managers can turn the unemployed over to the care of the State.)

Schematically, this approach had been tried out in Yanan with good results. Here "Self-Reliance", as practised by local collectives, found its full application. Tactically, the approach was fully in line with the principle of "walking on two legs", i.e. where the leg of modern technology was not available, the other had to step forward in the form of sheer massing of human muscular force plus the "innate inventiveness of the working masses". Execution of projects took on a distinctly military aspect, as frequently indicated by the terminology, such as that of an "extermination campaign" in which "superior numbers of people" "liquidated" a "contradiction" by "encircling and breaking down" the job into an infinite number of individual actions, like "ants nibbling a bone". Early visitors to such mass labour projects, such as the much-visited Ming Tomb Reservoir near Peking, returned, half awed, half appalled, by the sight of what they mistook for a dehumanized battle of "blue ants", in human shape, against nature.

All this gave rise to hideous misconceptions of slave labour driven on an unprecedented scale. A quotation such as the following is typical of this earlier misunderstanding: "The decision to embark upon the communisation programme is perhaps the Chinese Communists' biggest gamble to date. In treating the Chinese people callously, impersonally and ruthlessly, as raw material to be organized and manipulated by the state for its own purposes, they may be going too far, even for a totalitarian regime. ... It is not possible to predict the long-term reactions of the Chinese people. ... Nor can we know how the leaders of Communist China may react to pressures from the enslaved (54). ..." This one quotation is representative of many in the same vein. In the beginning, there must really have been some misunderstanding about the nature of the mass labour drives. But after the Chinese leadership had explained the circumstances and objectives of their utilization of mass labour, and knowledgeable foreign visitors - Edgar Snow, Claude Roy, Simone de Beauvoir, Keith Buchanan, René Dumont and many others - had given accurate descriptions of such projects, the continuing deprecation of human labour investment amounted to little else but slander. Periodically, as during the Great Leap or the Cultural Revolution, it was predicted that even if things had not yet become fully inhuman and unbearable, they were now growing so because of the increasing politicization of the drive. But the facts are far from having borne out such dire judgements.

In fact, the authorities did at first anticipate some reluctance from the peasants. The first projects were therefore advertised as revolutionary and patriotic endeavours for which volunteers were sought. Party members and members of the Young Communist League were expected to be the first to come forward and inspire the non-party masses by their example. The volunteers were grouped in quasi-military units, carried all their personal equipment on their shoulders like soldiers in a campaign, camped at the project site, were fed from military-type field kitchens, etc. All this set the style for the subsequent drives, when practically the entire labour force started to take turns in participating in Socialist Labour Campaigns. Nowadays, nobody - and particularly no cadres or other office-holders - can afford to let the call for volunteers go unheeded, although the apparently voluntary character of the operation is largely maintained. Women and girls form separate units but to a great extent assume the same tasks as men, including placing and detonating explosives, serving

---

54) A.D. Barnett, Communist China and Asia, A Challenge to American Policy, New York 1960, p.25.

as stone-masons in dangerous tunnels and on mountainsides, and so on.(55)

Large-scale projects became feasible as soon as the communes were able to muster large brigades of local manpower and to feed and supply them from the new commune canteens and supply stations. The camping units are otherwise self-reliant; their members have to learn to make do. ... At first they even had to manufacture their own tools, wheelbarrows, drilling apparatus, etc. Later, when mechanical equipment was no longer in desperately short supply, high-level political consultations decided that only part of the programme should henceforth be executed by mechanized forces, the large remainder being even in future reserved for sheer human labour "in order to teach the younger generation the merits of hard work, self-abnegation, mutual help and self-reliance" (56).

In this way it was calculated that on projects on light soils each worker moved an average of five cubic meters of earth a day, on heavy soils and mountain sites correspondingly less. Individual performances range from 30 to 120 work-days per year. Increasingly, work at socialist labour projects is combined with practical training in rare skills, such as drilling, concrete-pouring, rudimentary engineering, blasting, simple hydrology, etc. Over the years, the techniques of the labour gangs have become increasingly sophisticated and are passed on from shift to shift so that the project sites have become giant classrooms in the arts of manual labour and their most skillful use - preferably in combination with home-grown intermediate technologies and "ant nibbling a bone" techniques.

This has been closely linked with refinements in organizational techniques. Where projects were small, normally no major problems arose except that of dividing the task between brigades and teams. If, however, the project crosses commune boundaries, higher authorities take the initiative in bringing together the communes concerned in order to parcel out the workload and expected benefits in a fair way. Here, with the years, a great deal of experience, routine and confidence seems to have been gained. Things were not always so easy, especially when the communes were still poor and a great deal of communal labour burdened down the collectives' wage budgets. Here the State used an incentive, especially for large-scale projects where immediate advantages were not directly perceivable to the commune population. It sometimes

---

55) Report on female participation in the construction of the Red Flag Canal, China Today, Peking, 26.Oct.1974.
56) Henle, op. cit., Annex IX, p.240.

offered payment for the communes' labour contribution, mostly at a flat rate of one Yuan per man-day (57), in either kind (mostly foodgrains), or cash or both. For poorer communes this offered an assured and relatively highly remunerated way of income-earning, and their management committees were usually quite willing to hire out their redundant labour to the State. This approach, however, seems to have been only a first inducement; later on, as the communes grew more prosperous and learned what advantages the labour investment projects could bring to the community, the financial participation of the central authorities seems to have been gradually scaled down. Thus, State participation in such a major investment project as the Red Flag Canal, consisting mainly in deliveries of material, cement, explosives and drilling equipment and some construction steel, is reported to have come to 21.6% for the three main canals, but to only 1.5% if calculated for the entire 1500 km of the adduction and distribution network (58).

Resistance, if there was any, was largely overcome by the other unique feature of the commune system, the workday/work-point system of remuneration. Without it, peasants assigned to community infrastructure works could have complained with some justification that while their more fortunate neighbours were busy planting and harvesting bountiful crops, they had to sacrifice their labour for what was usually a pittance (the principle on which coolie labour had been founded). With the emergence of the socialist cooperatives and particularly the communes, these differentials were removed. Workers on communal jobs usually receive a flat work-day, or ten work-points, for each day worked. Thus, in principle, there is absolute equality in remuneration and it does not matter whether a person harvests rice fields, feeds pigs or digs an irrigation canal, his work-day being basically worth the same amount of points. Only the material value of each work-point - in cash and in kind - varies proportionally with the distributable product. Thus, proceeding from the principle of full employment for the entire labour force of a given collective, "labour time is regarded as a fixed factor, and any small addition it can make to output is considered worthwhile" (59), therefore productive, and consequently opening an entitlement to a proportionate share in the

---

57) Now increased to ¥ 1.50, see Khan, op.cit., p. 24.
58) Dumont, op. cit., p.124.
59) L.G. Reynolds, "China as a Less Developed Economy", American Economic Review, Vol.65, no.3, June 1975, p.424.

entire collective's gains. In this arrangement resides one key to the success of the Chinese system which is obviously not available to a free-market economy, whose enterprises are obliged to minimize operational costs and seek optimal economic equilibrium at the level not of the larger social unit but of their own.

In this way, communal manpower moved and/or installed a total of seventy billion cubic meters of earthwork and masonry between 1949 and 1960, "equivalent to 960 Suez Canals" (60) or 55 cubic meters of earth per year moved by each participant. But this was apparently only the prelude to much greater things to come, for one of the major objectives of the commune labour policies was to ensure that all available manpower was productively utilized. Thus, from the Great Leap Forward onward, many communes have kept labour teams at work on infrastructural projects throughout practically the entire year, although the strength of the teams varies and the persons deployed are rotated constantly. If transplanting or harvesting requires that all available manpower be in the fields, project work is interrupted, but otherwise all labour not needed in farm work, or in secondary functions such as communal industry, joins the manual labour gangs. These swell to gigantic armies once a year, when the winter season brings most other occupations to a halt. At the same time, the communal authorities are required to ensure that every person physically capable participates periodically. Thus, since 1960, each year not less than sixty million people, and since 1970 one hundred million people and often more (61), have turned out in each winter/spring period for socialist capital construction (62), averaging 60-100 work-days per person. This would yield a labour input ranging from 3.6 to 15 billion man-days/year. Dumont

---

60) State Statistical Bureau, Ten Great Years, Peking 1960, p.45.
61) In the winter of 1975/76, more than 130 million people participated in such mass labour projects (Hsinhua, Peking, 3 Nov.1976). In most communes, the output per person also rose prodigiously; thus, for instance, Pi Xian in Jiangsu reported in 1974 (Hongqi, no.1, Peking, Jan.1975, p.85) that the volume of earth moved in such projects in 1970-74 per person and year had often come near to one thousand cubic meters, a sure indication that the number of man-days spent in such projects must also have risen.
62) K.F. Hua, "Mobilizing the Whole Party...", Report at the Tachai Conference on Agriculture 1975, in Peking Review, No.44, 31 Oct.1975, p.7 et seq.

reports (63) that he was told that between fifteen and thirty percent of the communes' total annual labour expenditures during the last few years have been invested in mass-labour capital-creation projects.

It is tempting to try to assess more precisely the amount of labour invested in this type of "capital formation with bare hands", as the Chinese also sometimes call it. There are two possible approaches. The first would start from Dumont's indications and the assumption that China's rural labour force now numbers about 350 - 400 million persons. Assuming very roughly that their aggregate work input per year would be around 90 - 120 billion man-days and that 15% would be devoted to collective labour-intensive capital construction, one would arrive at 13.5 - 18 billion man-days - a staggering figure. The second approach would be based upon the annual announcements made through semi-official channels on the nationwide capital construction campaigns. For a number of years these statements give the total number of persons that participated. Sometimes even the average number of work-days per person has been indicated. Table 6 gives a compilation of aggregate numbers of participants and average numbers of work-days spent per person, estimated on the basis of Chinese statements:

Table 6

China's human mass labour investment 1964 - 1977

Year	number of persons (in mill.)	average no. of man-days per person
End of Consolidation period: (1964-65):	50-60	100
Average Third Plan (1966-70):	60-90	70-100
1970-71	100+	60-70
1971-72	110	60
1972-73	110-120	60-70
1973-74	130	70
1974-75	130-140	60
1975-76	150-160	50-60
1976-77	150+	60+

Source: Annual announcements by Hsinhua on aggregate national efforts in the past winter/spring capital construction campaigns.

63) Op. cit., p.58.

If the indications tabulated above are correct, the annual labour investment would have come to about 6 billion man-days per year by the end of the Consolidation period, to about 9 billion man-days by the end of the Third Plan, and to 9 - 10 billion man-days by the end of the Fourth Plan, but perhaps much more than that (63a).

From the viewpoint of accumulation and capital formation, these activities therefore play a role of the first order. Whatever the true value of the working day, it is certain that the mass-labour schemes each year contribute to China's national economic product and national wealth enormous fixed capital assets at no financial cost to the government, or with only a disproportionately small financial outlay. It can be assumed that the 3.6 to 15 billion man-days of annual investment in national capital formation is for the most part the non-monetary capitalization of China's otherwise unemployed labour force. Measuring the financial value of the contribution is difficult because the exact number and value of the objects thus created is not known. But it is almost certain that the valuation the Chinese government attaches to such contract labour remains considerably below the labour costs Western market economies would have to carry in the context of comparable projects. Also, if we examine the cost, in real terms, of similar objects erected in the West, such as the Tennessee Valley system, the St. Lawrence Waterway, etc., we will probably find not only that a great part of Western production costs other than labour was replaced in China by labour expended, but also that total costs per hectare reclaimed (in the case of land reclamation), or per HP or kW installed capacity (in the case of power stations), etc., are markedly lower in China. Thus it may safely be stated not only that effective accumulation and capital creation takes place but that Chinese equivalence rates between labour expended and material product created (average work-days expended: average cost per hectare irrigated, reclaimed, or HP installed capacity) have little relation to Western ones or to the fixed exchange rate between the Chinese Yuan (RMB) and the dollar.

This in turn raises an interesting point of accounting: the work-days expended were remunerated by the sponsoring collectives with a corresponding number of work-

---

63a) The estimates given by Nickum (J.E. Nickum, The use of labour-intensive techniques for rural public works in the PRC, OECD, Paris 1975) are most probably too low because they tend to discount Chinese statements about the number of annual participants, sometimes by as much as 50%.

days/points. Assuming that the annual aggregate value of these work-days, at the rate of one Yuan, has been 3.6 to 15 billion Y, it is noteworthy that no equivalent additional purchasing power is pumped into the national economy, because the work-points are honoured exclusively from the cash and commodity product of the collectives, which would have been earned or harvested in any case. Hence, absence of inflationary pressure upon the market stemming from wage payments for this additional employment of surplus labour; hence, no nominal increase in the monetary supply emerging as countervalue to the material value created by the labour input; hence, assets seemingly obtained without paying a price (actually paid by the materially productive members of the collective whose share in the collective product is diminished correspondingly); hence, no real monetary price although national wealth and domestic product increase. (63b)

But by how much? Since the State budget was only marginally involved if at all, and by no means proportionately to the value a market economy would attach to the created asset, the increment must be measured in what by foreign standards is an arbitrary and artificial valuation, by the number of working days expended - monetized for convenience' sake at one Yuan. As a result, an enormous undervaluation will appear when the assets created are entered into the national product accounts, as indeed seems to take place on the basis of the few available reports on this point. Hence, an ineluctable underestimation of China's real economic performance in the infrastructural capital sector.

Objects of such capital construction by labour investment are to be found throughout the entire rural economy. Two sectors, however, were selected for priority treatment: irrigation, water conservation and hydrological management; and soil and topological improvement. Government instructions on water conservation directed the communes to prefer small-scale projects to big ones and water conservation and storage to diversion. As a result, 2.3 million small reservoirs have been built in the Huangho valley, more than one million in Guangdong province, etc., and these serve today to retain excess rain and flood water and make it available for irrigation.

63b) This viewpoint is indirectly supported by recent Chinese information (Le Monde, 30 Sept.1977) according to which a general increase in wage and salary levels has become overdue, as money supply doubled (over what time? apparently between 1962 and 1977) while goods supply increased nearly five times.

Extensive irrigation canal networks were dug, enabling vast areas to proceed from single to double-cropping and in South China to triple-cropping. At the same time, the vulnerability of the countryside to drought, flooding and typhoons in the South was decisively lowered.

Soil improvement concentrated on the collection and relocation of precious topsoil in areas where erosion and karst formation have lowered soil quality. Fields are freed from stones and boulders, leveled and graded to allow drainage of excess water, and are terraced in hill areas. Hills are leveled. The Tachai brigade alone flattened thirty-one hillocks on its territory between 1958 and 1972 and turned them into fields (64). With a view to mechanization, small plots are consolidated into so-called mini-plains to allow the rational use of tractors for ploughing, harrowing, etc. A typical approach, combining collective work with the course of nature, is the echeloned creation of mini-plains by silting. In narrow valleys, erosion and outflow gullies are closed up by check dams, against which rain torrents are allowed to deposit their sediments carried from the slopes. In narrow valleys, six to fourteen such check dams, between two and eight meters high, depending on the topography, are installed per sqkm and allowed to fill up and silt in completely in ten years, with a gain of 2 to 3.5 hectares of new crop land. Later, the small plots are merged into larger units. In larger valleys, higher and wider dams of ten to twenty meters are erected, often only two to four per sqkm, and the resulting silting creates proportionally larger areas. These dams are built by labour parties of 15 to 150 peasants in 10 to 120 days, entirely with local hand tools. After about ten years of silting, the second stage of soil improvement, levelling, etc., begins.

Even in the short run, the results of such land improvement works in terms of increasing crop output appear to be very impressive. Chinese governmental sources say that already after one to three years of terracing work in North China's loess area, the effects of enhanced water retention in the soil, of soil enrichment with nutrients otherwise easily leached out, and of accumulating humus and silt on the surface are so considerable that crop yields rise by 100 to 300 %. Terracing conducted up to what the Chinese call the stage of "Tachai fields" is said to reduce water loss by 90% and more, silt loss by 85% to 95%, especially after heavy rains, and nutrient loss by 65 to 75% (65).

---

64) H.W. Hsin, *Tachai, Standard-bearer in China's Agriculture,* Peking 1972, p.12.

65) Ministry of Irrigation and Water Control, op.cit.,p.208 et seq.

All this shows that there is a close correlation indeed between sheer hard work and very tangible improvements in land productivity, harvest volume, food supplies and ultimately, food security. Here lies a lesson on which the majority of those underdeveloped countries which are so quick in running to the world bodies clamouring for more aid and handouts of even basic commodities, would do well to meditate profoundly. For here it is shown that even under the poorest of environmental and physical conditions an oversized but determined labour force, self-reliant, well-led, persistent, can master even the most overwhelming odds against self-sustained economic growth - without any machinery, any outside aid, any World Bank loans, provided the spirit is the correct one. Where do all those receivers of billions of development aid stand in comparison?

All this explains how such socialist labour projects directly serve agriculture and why the Chinese insist that the real increases in land unit productivity have just begun and can be carried much further. It also serves to refute earlier views denying the labour-intensive projects any significance but that of politically motivated schemes for creating employment, without any real economic impact.

At the same time, the results of this approach to capital construction over time have become visible and, in the shape of increasing yields, tangible to the Chinese villagers. They can therefore be assumed to act as a strong incentive for them to participate in more such projects. But this alone does not fully explain how the Chinese won the active and persistent support of their village population, particularly at the beginning of this arduous endeavour. The answer to this question is probably a double one: not only economic but political motivation; and organization.

As for motivation, the existence of a tangible material incentive for the villagers to participate in collective labour has been shown. It consists in the triple guarantee of work, income for this work and an egalitarian system of remuneration based exclusively on the amount of work performed. The Chinese authorities have consistently encouraged the population to conceptualize these as advantages gained by political reforms and only secondarily as resulting merely from material progress. Emphasis is placed on building a better, more just, more egalitarian socialist society, on "improving the motherland" and on transforming it "by revolution". Engaging in capital construction is part of changing, bettering the physical substratum, therefore revolution in the true Marxist sense. Here no task is too great, no obstacle insurmountable, no personal sacrifice vain, not in chasing after abstract ideals but in making tangible improvements for society as a whole. This is the message propounded by the three texts which are continually proposed for study: Serve the People, In Memory of Norman Bethune and The Foolish Old Man Who Removed the Mountain, all early essays by Chairman Mao and going back to the Yanan days. Their daily study and discussion forms part of the curricula of the labour investment teams which are thus led to realize that, exploitation and private appropriation of surplus value having been abolished in the new society, there is no reason for not going all-out to create the material conditions for "more and more and better and better" for the entire society.

In particular, the private appropriation of the fruits of communal labour is, as is well known from many other developing countries, a strong disincentive to efforts by the rural population to improve their condition. It has often been reported, (66) for example from India, how entire villages refused to contribute to such improvement works as the digging of irrigation canals, even if offered part payment in the form of food. They explained that although such irrigation work, the fruit of labour undertaken jointly, would certainly increase crop yields, they saw no point in it as it would merely permit the landlord to increase the land rent; they would not undertake anything that would be of primary benefit to the landowners. Reports from many other developing countries where private cultivation still prevails confirm the survival of this attitude. Chinese collectivization consequently removed an important psychological stumbling block.

Organization is provided by the CCP, whose cadres have to provide living examples and lead the way, not so much technically - although on the lowest levels this also is part of their task - but humanly and politically, so that the once amorphous, inarticulate masses of labourers are broken down into small cells of motivated, conscious participants who as individuals actively grasp the collective goal. Again the emphasis is on political conceptualization. When it is there, technical comprehension of the task and of the best ways to go about it will follow ineluctably. Wherever participating workers are not yet fully up to it, the cadre has to work along with them, explain, reason until the energizing effect has been reached.

In fact this very close symbiotic relationship between the labour force and the cadres or, as one would say in the

---

66) See for example: R.Segal, The Crisis of India, London 1962, p.163 et seq.

Occident, "the managers", is considered by the Chinese a key to the success of their social and economic model. The Chinese leadership has insisted again and again that cadres must not only direct and instruct but share the workforce's toil and sweat as their own living experience. Only then are they able to lead with authority, to find the right answers to the problems of the instant and to wrest success from overwhelmingly adverse conditions. Already during the Yanan days, cadres were instructed to practise the "Three Togethers" - work together, eat together, sleep together with the labouring masses in order to become one with them, to see their problems as they see them. Later, during the Cultural Revolution, instructions went out that xian cadres had to do at least a hundred days a year of manual labour in their parish, commune cadres two hundred days and brigade cadres three hundred days. This norm was often exceeded. Thus, a particularly successful xian, Bei Xian in Jiangsu, reported in 1974 that its commune cadres had performed manual labour of an average of 264 days a year (67) - in its eyes a clear reason why it was so successful. (67a) This part of the Chinese approach and the role of the party and its cadres have been so far too little observed, analyzed and translated into terms that the ideologically uncommitted outside world can comprehend, but all indications suggest that here resides one essential ingredient to the success of the Chinese experiment in mass labour organization.

In this context, Stavis (67a) raised the highly interesting question whether the difference in course and outcome between the Soviet and the Chinese rural collectivization drives should not be primarily explained by the fact that the Soviet countryside in the late 1920s was simply understaffed with party cadres capable of leading the peasants into the collectives in an orderly, humanly acceptable way. Lack of cadres and party organization in the villages may have forced the Soviet Communist Party (CPSU) into what the Chinese call "commandism" - brusque orders backed up by police force. The following facts and figures are in any case highly instructive: In 1929, only 310,000 or 21% of all Soviet party members lived in the villages. In China in 1955, the number of rural party members was about 4 million, or 43% of the total membership. Thus the average number of party workers per 1,000 village inhabitants was 2.7 in the U.S.S.R. on the eve of

---

67) Hongqi No.1, Peking, January 1975, pp.83-86.
67a) See B. Stavis, The Impact of Agricultural Collectivization upon Productivity in China, Ithaca, N.Y., 1977, p.20.

collectivization but 7.5 in China in 1955. The percentage of villages with a party organization in the U.S.S.R. of 1929 was 33-39%, depending on the definition, but 77% in China. For those observers who have seen CPC cadres at work in their villages, these figures tell an impressive story indeed.

A good example of what has been accomplished by mass labour investment methods is the Haihe River Control project (68), covering about 265,000 sqkm and involving parts of Hebei, Shanxi, Shandong and Henan provinces and the two Municipal Regions of Peking and Tianjin. The first small sub-projects, mostly for water conservation and the construction of dykes and drainage canals, were undertaken in 1950 and continued until 1963, when a comprehensive master plan was completed. In the following eight years the Haihe river bed was widened and deepened over a length of 80 km, so that river traffic by strings of barges became possible; 26 major canals totalling 2,160 km were dug, and 25 major dykes of a total length of 2,340 km were erected. There are four major sea sluices and flood basins and 19 new secondary river outlets to the sea, with 1,600 km of new river bed. The number of bridges and minor floodgates in 1972 exceeded 50,000. The total volume of earth moved was 1.9 billion cubic meters. Ancillary work in the watershed areas created eleven large hydroelectric dams, 26 medium dams and more than 1,000 small reservoirs, allowing 988,000 hectares of waste land to be reclaimed for cultivation, and protecting 3.3 million hectares of farm land from water-logging. In Hebei province alone, more than 200,000 wells were sunk and 230,000 hectares were reforested, and the province thus became self-sufficient in grain supplies.

This workload was executed by mass labour mobilizing 300,000 to 400,000 persons each winter at the main sites and one to two million at ancillary projects. The annual labour input on the major sub-projects exceeded 45 million man-days a year.

The manpower strategy used in executing the scheme was described as follows: Each individual project component was classified into one of three groups:

- those to be executed by collective labour in collaboration with State teams for specialized work, such as excavation teams, cement pourers, etc.;

---

68) Cf. Henle, op.cit. Annex IX, p.238 et seq.; Communications from the Haiho River Authority, Tianjin, June 1972. Also see C. Ho, Harm into Benefit: Taming the Haiho River, Peking 1975.

- those requiring mainly collective labour, with only little technical support from the State;
- subsidiary projects to be carried out exclusively by collective labour.

Each job was then assigned to a commune or group of communes (or brigades of urban labour), which had to organize the work and complete it within an established time schedule. If technical advice or cooperation was needed, the State would provide it, subject to the concurrence of the overall planning authority, the Haihe River Administration in Tianjin. Then "enough and more than enough forces" were rapidly concentrated in "an annihilation campaign" upon one sub-project at a time, so that the work could be finished in a relatively short period, such as one winter season. Very heavy emphasis was laid on the completion of all parts of a sub-project simultaneously or in rapid sequence, so that no work was left idle or half-finished for extended periods before it could be put into service. As far as possible, planning and working were unified. Workers, brought from their homes on foot, worked with their everyday work tools, shovels, hoes, shoulder poles, etc., "in order to teach the people the spirit of fighting, endurance, improvization". In later stages, from 1966 or 1967 onward, when enough trucks, tractors and excavators had become available in the State machine parks, the question whether labour-intensive methods should be maintained or abandoned, was discussed on several levels. The policy decision was that in future, 50% of the workload should be carried by mass labour and the other half by mechanized methods but supported by mass labour, in order to conserve the educational value of the mass labour approach.

Characteristically, the Haihe River Administration stated in 1972 that no overall cost/benefit assessment had been made. However, some accounts for sub-projects had been drawn up. The Zuya Canal complex, one of the major new waterways combined with drainage and irrigation main canals, 143 km long, with over 200 bridges and floodgates, several power stations and many other ancillary objects, had been assessed at about sixty million Yuan, about equal to the outlay from the State budget. It had been constructed by more than 300,000 workers in five months.

Another major, but more specialized, field of mass labour application is forestry. Almost immediately after Liberation, the Chinese authorities being aware of the fundamental importance of a healthy balance between forest cover and cultivation area, and the country's crying need for massive reforestation, the government initiated first small, then larger and larger afforestation drives. In the Great Leap Forward, the annual area worked or reworked for forestry rose to well over ten million hectares. Much of this had to be replanted several times, but there is no doubt that the forest cover expanded considerably, to the greatest extent thanks to the use of communal manpower.

These afforestation drives were carried forward simultaneously on several levels:

- on the village level by creating village and fuelwood plantations for local use;

- on the commune level by planting shelterbelts, wind rows and tree screens to protect crop fields against wind erosion, dust storms in the North, encroachments by wandering desert dunes; in headwater areas and on denuded slopes by planting protection forests which (as in Shanxi and Shaanxi) have changed the entire topological aspect of many areas;

- on the xian level in the South and Centre, by regenerating stands of precious species for industrial use.

Some of these projects involved millions of hectares. The total forest cover of China was stated by semi-official sources to have increased to "more than twice the area under forest at Liberation" (69), which would bring it to 150 to 160 million ha, if the official base figure for 1949 is adopted.

Manpower investment in afforestation projects has the peculiarity of initially calling for very high labour inputs. Depending on soil condition and topological circumstances, requirements of 200 to 500 man-days per hectare have been mentioned in various provinces of China for the principal phase of the projects, the planting of seedlings, although in some cases the figures include the preparation of the planting beds while others exclude this. Requirements then decline immediately until the stands mature. Consequently, if the effort is maintained over a sufficiently long period, large areas can eventually be brought under reforestation - and this is what the Chinese aim at doing in order to restore an ecologically satisfactory balance between cropland, pasture and forest and to obtain a consequential improvement in soil moisture, rainfall and climate. Over time, the communal reforestation programme within the framework of mass labour investment schemes is one of the most important long-term endeavours undertaken in the Chinese countryside since Liberation.

---

69) Hsinhua, Peking, 15 Nov.1975.

Labour supply to state industry

Apart from the three-pronged policy of creating rural employment inside and outside agriculture, the commune sector must and does supply labour to the urban industrial and generally non-rural sector, and will continue to do so. No hard data or other detailed information are available concerning the last fifteen years, but there are many indications that this flow continues, although on a much reduced scale. The composition of the force transferred, however, seems to have changed. Instead of large numbers of unskilled labourers for the city-wide or inter-industrial labour pools, the migrants now tend to be pre-trained and at least partly qualified skilled workers from commune industries or commune and xian machine/tractor stations. It has been stated (70) that China's rural sector now possesses over ten million fully-trained specialists in farm mechanization on whom China's industry can fall back in case of a manpower squeeze.

The authorities seem determined to keep the outflow as low as possible, not only by sponging up all available manpower in the cities themselves - a stage which seems for the most part to have been passed long ago - but also by dissociating industrialization from urbanization. Wherever possible, manpower is not brought to the industrial agglomerations, but industry is installed where manpower is available, provided, of course, that there is no conflict with other factors important from the standpoint of location. It is frequent for well-established urban industrial enterprises, especially along the eastern seabord, to limit deliberately their own expansion in favour of setting up new subsidiaries further inland in communes and xian. These new branch enterprises receive a steady flow of support in the form of skilled personnel, second-hand equipment from the main plant and blueprints and production plans. Moreover, many entire enterprises have been rusticated when their backward and forward linkages to suppliers and clients permitted or when satisfactory alternatives could be established.

Furthermore, two other specific programmes directly counter the flow of rural labour to the cities. The first is the Xiafang movement, under which town-based cadres and specialists are routinely "sent down" (the literal translation of the Chinese term) to the villages for stays of variable duration, from a few months to a few years. The main purpose of the scheme, however, is directly related not to labour but rather to social policies: to bring people in

---

70) Hsinhua, Peking, 15 Nov.1975.

privileged or functionally isolated positions periodically back into existential contact with the living reality of the toiling masses, to show them how four fifths of the Chinese people live and think and what their problems are, and to correct their own outlook and social self-identification by manual labour or, as the Chinese put it, "to put them back into the proletarian mould". Nonetheless, the corollary of the Xiafang displacement of cadres is that sizeable numbers of highly qualified specialists from all professional walks of life are brought back to the villages to live and contribute to production there.

Similar, but much more closely linked to strategies of economic construction and employment, is the annual wave of migration of qualified youths from the cities and the East to the thinly populated and underdeveloped provinces of the North and West and the interior generally. Thus, between 1956 and 1965, about fifteen million (71) young city dwellers, mostly middle and high school graduates, were called upon to volunteer for permanent settlement in the new areas. The figure for the years 1966 to 1972 was estimated (72) to be near ten million. Thus an average of 260,000 youngsters per year were funnelled to Xinjiang, 150,000 to Inner Mongolia, 80,000 to Tibet, 60,000 to Heilongjiang and Jilin, 30,000 to Qinghai. Official sources stress the cultural interpenetration: "a kind of educational fertilization of the countryside" occurs when such large numbers of educated, skilled youths are settled among backward villagers (73). The new arrivals usually form the spearhead of drives for innovation and technical reform in all sectors.

Impact on China's agriculture and food production

In summing up the results so far perceivable of China's three-pronged strategy of absorbing rural manpower surpluses and "turning consumers into producers", it is fitting to examine its repercussions upon China's traditionally foremost indicator of economic success or failure: food production and nutritional standards. It is generally known that between Liberation and the end of the Fourth Plan, output of foodgrains increased by more than 150%. The increase during the First Plan was steady - from 108 mil-

---

71) L. Orleans, Every Fifth Child: the Population of China, London 1972, p.104.
72) Peking Review, No.52, 28 Dec.1974, p.19.
73) Renmin Ribao, Peking, 28 Oct.1972.

lion tons (unified grain equivalent) in 1949 to 185 million (U.G.E.) in 1957. Actual performance during the first years of the Great Leap is still subject to debate, but there is little doubt that it was marked by large advances. These latter in turn were succeeded during the Calamity Years of 1960-62 by as great or even greater setbacks, the exact figures for which are also not yet known. For the following years only confidential indications (such as those reported by Burki and Swami) (74) and approximate calculations are available. Official Chinese figures were published again only for the last year of the Third Plan, 1970, for which the harvest was given as being 240 million tons (U.G.E.). This figure and the following ones are no longer comparable to those published for 1949-59, because the definition of unified grain equivalent had been changed in the meantime, apparently several times and each time in a more restrictive sense. Roughly speaking, it may be said that the 240 million tons of 1970 represented much more in real produce than the officially announced 250 million tons of 1958, and all the more so since the latter may in reality have amounted to only 220 million tons.

To recapitulate well-known facts just one step further: the official harvest figures from 1970 onward are given in Table 7.

Table 7

China's foodgrain production 1970 - 1976

Year	Million tons (U.G.E.)
1970	240
1971	250
1972	242
1973	258 *
1974	275
1975	283 *
1976	293 *

* = unofficial and preliminary

Sources:
Various governmental announcements as reported by Hsinhua and unofficial estimates.

---

74) For these and preceding data, see inter alia: S. Swamy and S.J. Burki, "Foodgrains Output in the People's Republic of China, 1958-65", in The China Quarterly, No.41, London, Jan.1970, pp.58-63.

The table above shows that during the Fourth Plan, China's grain production increased by about 17%, or an annual average of 3 to 3.5%. At a time when world increase rates in food production hovered around 2% and in the Third World even below that level, this is a very honourable performance. It is all the more significant as it outpaced population growth by at least double. In other words, on the basis of the 1970-1975 performances, China no longer has to fear the Malthusian menace of a population outgrowing its food supply; on the contrary, the nutritional standards of the population are actually improving year after year by a relatively secure margin. This is a success very few other developing countries can claim.

It is the more impressive as China, in respect of land development, land and soil utilization and unused land reserve, is not a "developing" (in the sense of "new") country at all but a very ancient one whose soil and land reserves, as has been seen in Chapter 1, had been over-exploited for centuries. The country had long since suffered greatly from the gradual exhaustion of its soil and the degradation of much of its productive area. When the Communists began their agrarian development drive there was little question of ploughing virgin ground and sowing into untouched soil: they had to start from an already tense basic situation. Their achievement is therefore all the more striking.

How was it done, and what role was played by the strategies described earlier in this chapter? Very little is still known about the Chinese development model and its gradual elaboration, which would deserve a more comprehensive study in itself. But insofar as it is relevant here, the following can be said in brief:

One first and constant objective was and is the expansion of the productive basis. It was to be extended outward, i.e. by continuous efforts toward land reclamation and the opening up of sub-standard areas. Some of the results attained during the Third and Fourth Plans have already been noted. According to unofficial reports [75] the arable area had reached 127 million ha in 1972, and Japanese sources reported in 1975 that in the latter year it had been brought to about 133 to 135 million ha. All this was achieved by decentralized labour-intensive methods, the only ones available to China, for any alternative approach would have cost her the equivalent of one or several Marshall Plans in capital, which clearly was not available.

---

75) Henle, op. cit., p.91.

Impact on agriculture and food production

At the same time, expansion was directed to go "upward" by means of soil improvement, terracing, soil protection and similar measures. A quantification of the immense efforts that went into this direction is more difficult. In the absence of comprehensive official data, an approximate yardstick would lie in the increases of yield, but here again it is difficult to disaggregate soil improvement effects from other factors. Again it must be stressed that practically all achievements in this field were accomplished by commune labour in the form of labour investment projects.

Closely connected with this is the strategy of advancing "in multiple tiers", i.e. by intensification of multiple-cropping. Climatically, most of intra-mural China (south and east of the Great Wall) is naturally suited for more than one crop per year, the growing season being long enough. Even southern and central Manchuria and areas in the Far West have enough frost-free days to put in more than one crop. What in the past had prevented these regions from doing so was mainly the lack of water. Here the tremendous efforts to set up an infrastructural network to control the water economy of the country, from huge river dams down to the several millions of small storage reservoirs and underground cisterns collecting rainwater and checking floods, have contributed immensely to making available the necessary irrigation to compensate even for extended periods of drought (e.g. ninety days in Guangdong). According to official Chinese communications, between half and two thirds of China's cultivated area are now under "full irrigation" or have drainage facilities (76), while according to an American observer, (77) about 95% of all areas appear to have access to some adducted water. Again, practically all of the immense water control works were executed by rural manual labour.

At the same time, the Chinese government concentrated upon yield improvement. The Chinese started their own Green Revolution about ten years before the West was ready for it. The first improved varieties of rice were generalized by the University of Nanking in 1952, in the lower Yangtze valley (77a). Genetic work was so intensive that the entire genetic stock of the major crop categories has been renewed completely at least three times since Liberation. Characteristically, in the beginning the Chinese

---

76) Hsinhua, Peking, 23 Oct.1975.
77) S.Y. Wu, "A Report on the Chinese Commune", in Chinese Chinese Economic Studies, Vol.VIII, no.3, White Plains, N.Y., 1975, p.83.
77a) Henle, op. cit., p. 144.

aimed not so much at increases in yield as at resistance to cold, drought and windbreak. Greater fruit weight was bred in only later. But the improved resistance properties allowed Chinese agronomists to extend rice cultivation northward from the Huanghe valley deep into Manchuria, summer and even winter wheat into Tibet, winter wheat southward into Guangxi and Hainan, maize into Xinjiang, Ningxia and Manchuria, etc. Simultaneously, the new varieties, owing to their photo-period insensitivity, have considerably shorter maturing periods. The ripening time for rice, for example, was reduced from 130-140 days to 90-100. This again allowed better use of the growing period, two short-period crops replacing one of longer duration. In northern China, in order to win even more time, not only is rice now preplanted and then transplanted, but some communes are now doing the same with wheat, gaining one additional wheat crop. All this, of course, is possible only thanks to immensely increased labour inputs into agricultural work. Similar innovations apply to the extension of intercropping and overlap cultivation, so that the Chinese can soon speak of having triple-cropping in most areas south of the Yangtze. Some communes in Guangdong, with intensive market farming, have attained a total of twelve harvests a year of vegetables, fruit and cash crops.

If the high yielding varieties (HYVs) need sufficient and stable supplies of irrigation water above all, their full yield potential comes out only under adequate fertilization. Foodgrain HYVs surpass traditional seed varieties three to four times in yield, provided not only water but also chemical fertilizer is applied in three to four times greater quantities. Experimentally, the optimal amounts of all types of chemical fertilizer were determined as lying between 170 and 200 kg/ha (nutrient) per grain crop. Present supplies in China are still far from having reached this level, especially for two or three crops per year, but there is no doubt that the availability of much greater quantities of plant nutrients has contributed decisively to the impressive output increases since the lean days of the Calamity Years. Here again, the existence of a widespread rural fertilizer industry has been instrumental in helping the commune farmers to achieve the yield increases which are more and more common: 3.1 tons/ha of winter wheat in Tibet, 7.5 to 12 tons/ha of early wet rice in the lower Yangtze valley, 12 to 15 tons/ha of tubers in South China, etc.

The concerted Chinese advance in all sectors of the agricultural production process is thus beginning to pay its dividends. Considerable production increases have begun to come in, but this is an ongoing process: much more can be expected, and the Chinese, probably correctly, point out that the really big quantitative progress is still to come.

Rural capital supply

Another very positive aspect of the communal system of turning labour into capital is the way in which the rural collectives not only have become financially increasingly liquid but have been so strengthened as to enable them to relieve the central fiscal bodies of a wide and costly range of financial tasks in the agricultural sector. This contrasts strongly with conditions before Liberation, when China's farming community was notoriously impecunious, and therefore to a very large extent constantly in the clutches of rural money-lenders who drained all the surplus, only to invest it in refuge values such as gold, conspicuous consumption or urban mercantile speculation even if they did not simply buy up land, inflating land values and leading to the eviction of poor farmers (78). Such a situation is no longer conceivable in China. But not only are such savings now put to good economic use: they are no longer funnelled into governmental fiscal coffers but remain in the villages, where they are generated, and are invested there.

These are not abstract macro-economic ruminations but realities that express themselves in daily economic life. The communes' own credit cooperatives that manage the collectives' operational liquidities and reserve funds as well as the individual members' savings accounts, are, after some initial hesitations and errors, doing remarkably well. In 1973, more than 60% of these commune credit co-ops were able to provide their parent collectives with all the loan capital they required to meet their current obligations and investment needs under the Plan (79). Where local credit co-ops were not able to provide all the funds needed, many communes could cover the difference by turning to

---

78) This situation still prevails in most other developing countries. In India, for example, it was estimated that in 1968 the annual equivalent of at least US$ 4,000 million was being invested in gold and ornaments by rural Banyas, Marwaris (merchants, money-lenders), landlords and rich peasants, hoarded and thus withdrawn from the economic circuit (Times of India, Bombay, 2 Dec.1969).

79) Renmin Ribao, Peking, 21 Nov.1974.

their _xian_, and more precisely to the _xian_ branches of the People's Bank. As the _xian_, and with them their financial institutions, may still be considered part of the rural sector, it can be concluded that the large majority of China's communes obtain their financial supply out of their own reserves, that is, that they have become truly self-reliant with regard to financing. The tremendous difficulties that arise in organizing a reliable rural credit system in underdeveloped countries represent a measure of the Chinese achievement. In India, for example, rural institutional credit reaches hardly more than 10 to 15% of the small and middle farmers, and large proportions of agricultural loans are never recovered (in Karnataka, Tamil Nadu and Andhra Pradesh an average 35% of the total volume in the 1960s (80)), so that here as elsewhere agricultural financing is a constant bottomless barrel for the State's resources.

---

80) Financial Express, Bombay, 5 July 1970.

CHAPTER VII

Mechanization and Future Outlook

While agriculture and food production in particular take first place in the hierarchy of China's rural development goals and therefore have absolute priority in the allocation of manpower, it is expressly foreseen that agriculture will have to take steps progressively to rationalize labour utilization. Not only will industrialization and greater diversification of the economy absorb greater quantities of manpower, but advancing intensification of agricultural production itself depends on more productive labour inputs and therefore on more rational use of labour. The Chinese themselves recognized early that this can be achieved by greater use of mechanization.

Here again, the collective nature of Chinese farming draws the course to follow and sets the limitations to the mechanization strategy. Mechanization in the communes cannot proceed in a way that may lead to an excess of social costs - such as redundancy of field labour, lowering of wages, migration of unemployed - over private benefits. As there are no private owners or entrepreneurs, only social benefits and/or costs are determinant for the speed and course of the introduction of machinery. When crop work is mechanized, the entire collective must, in some way or other, benefit, be it from lessened toil, reduced labour intensity, increases in income or greater job diversification. Workers who become redundant in one function must be immediately provided with another one. The dire social consequences of mechanization, as e.g. in India, such as massive unemployment, eviction of tenants, lowering of wage incomes, while the owners of land and tractors increase their profits, are completely precluded. Inversely, a commune will mechanize to such an extent that the available local manpower no longer suffices to cope with the workload at hand; that management perceives opportunities to increase output, e.g. by shortening the time span between the beginning of the harvest of an early crop and the potential planting of a late one so that the unit can proceed from single- to double-cropping; or that the suffering and hardship of manual work can be avoided. Mere savings in human labour themselves are no incentive towards mechanization, only if the manpower set free is needed elsewhere, for instance in new commune industry. The availability of financial resources, be it from the commune's own accumulation fund, be it in the form of a credit from the People's Bank of the xian, acts as the one major constraint.

Definition of mechanization

Mechanization, as the Chinese use the term, implies more than the introduction of tractors and other mobile gear in crop work. It essentially includes electrification of most productive work at the village level, the motorization of such hugely labour-consuming tasks as water pumping; other stationary mechanization; and motorization of transport at the commune and even brigade levels. In addition to ploughing, cultivation, harvesting and food processing, "basic mechanization", the term hitherto most often used by the Chinese, further covers the motorization of basic functions in forestry, land improvement, animal husbandry and fisheries. The concept is thus presented in the broadest possible terms.

Another term, "selective mechanization", denotes a general approach: after initial trials and some tractorization of field work, local collectives were mainly left to choose for themselves the sectors of their activities that needed the earliest introduction of mechanical power. Consequently, they were allowed to go about it in function of the priorities they themselves defined. There was no country-wide and uniform strategy, for instance to start everywhere with tractorization, then to move into mechanization of irrigation, etc., but many varieties of approaches.

Historically, economies in manpower were not the Chinese's first and foremost aim in mechanization. At the outset, mechanization was seen as permitting the gradual abolition of physically exhausting, backbreaking toil, or the "three bendings" - in carrying and pumping, in transplanting and in harvesting - in order to lighten the physical stress of farm work. A second aspect was added early during the pre-Leap years: the shortening of certain critical phases of crop work, for example in order to make use of the short growing and harvesting seasons in the North, with its few frost-free days. Reducing labour requirements became a vital issue only when the labour reserves at the commune level were increasingly subjected to simultaneous and conflicting claims. This had been foreseen as being eventually inevitable, but institutional improvements and better management techniques were expected to stretch the period of transition and actually did, if the productivity levels attained in China are compared with those in other Asian countries where mechanization has also begun.

Mechanization, as in the early U.S.S.R., initially was not so much a device to raise labour productivity as a tangible symbol of modernization and enlightenment for the rural masses. Lenin's dictum, "Electrification plus peasants' councils equal communism in the villages", was paraphrased many times in China during the Yanan and early Reconstruction days. Mechanization was explicitly mentioned in the National (Twelve-Year) Plan for Agricultural Development as an ultimate goal and indispensable ingredient of truly socialist production relationships, but subject to prior successful institutional and motivational changes. A policy statement issued by the government at the height of the Great Leap Forward discussed the correct approach to increases in labour productivity as follows: "One way is by increasing the enthusiasm of man for labour. This requires ... the development of the spirit that leads man to exert his utmost. ... There is, however, a limit to this way of increasing the rate of productivity of agricultural labour. ... The only fundamental way to raise it ... beyond (human and institutional limits of improvement) is by the gradual realization of mechanization and electrification. ... This is what our party is striving for ... "(81). Thus, even at that relatively early stage, institutional reform, improved human motivations and mechanization were for the Chinese not alternatives implying different degrees of political and economic desirability and expediency but mutually interrelated components of a single comprehensive development strategy.

The three-stage strategy

According to the earlier plans, mechanization was to proceed in three stages. The first concentrated on a selective approach with emphasis upon the most urgently needed forms of additional energy, e.g., mechanizing the water supply and drainage as the keys to yield improvement and multiple cropping, and on "semi-mechanizing" crop work by introducing improved tools and simple machines of intermediate technology. Semi-mechanization was and still is a field of predilection for practising "Walking on Two

---

81) <u>Renmin Ribao</u>, Peking, 12 March 1959.

Legs" policies and applying the "Mass Line", i. e., making use of farmers' experience and giving free rein to the innate inventiveness and initiatives of the population. The Chinese leadership, contrary to that of most other developing countries, thus took a positive attitude towards the many local make-do practices and devices and encouraged their use and extension as much as possible. During and after the Great Leap an immense number of such intermediate-level inventions appeared, often decisively helping in local development.

Little attempt was made at standardizing the immense host of make-do devices, simple machines and contraptions which cropped up everywhere in the villages, although the best were carefully analyzed and if found useful, their plans distributed in the xian, the diqu or even nation-wide, as models to follow. To this group belong the "Dragon Chain" (a conveyor-belt device carrying buckets for water pumping), the "Liberation Water Wheel" (iron discs on an endless chain carrying water upward through a tight-fitting pipe) and the many types of rice transplanters now in use. One, developed in Shandong and heralded throughout the country, costs about 1,000 ¥. Operated by three men, it transplants six to eight mou in four hours, the amount twenty-four men can do by hand in the same time. Although this machine is highly labour-saving, the real reason for the authorities to have encouraged its introduction in northern rice-growing areas is that the machine shortens the critical time for transplanting seedlings for a second, late rice crop after the early summer rice has been harvested, thus permitting a second harvest in areas where previously only one was possible (82).

Among other achievements was the wide introduction of the windmill, threshers, huskers, crushers, cable-ways and cable traction for ploughing, disc ploughs, etc., all very successfully manufactured ever since by communal factories. Semi-mechanization is not seen as a substitute for full mechanization, but in Chinese eyes it is bound to endure and has its place to supplement the latter and to be further developed simultaneously with it.

The second stage foresaw the full mechanization of selected areas whose growing potential could be fully utilized only by use of mechanical equipment, e.g. the Northeast, where the maximum time interval the climate allows between the ripening of winter grain and the last feasible date for the sowing or transplanting of an autumn crop is 15 to 20 days. Only through the intensive use of harvesters and tractorized ploughs can all the necessary

---

82) Hsinhua, Peking, 24 May 1974.

operations be compressed into so short a period. Therefore, already by 1970, more than 75% of the northern and central Manchurian fields were being worked by "big machines". Elsewhere, mechanization was being prepared by the creation of large contiguous units, in the plains of ten, twenty and more hectares surrounded by shelterbelts, in the hills and uplands of one to five hectares by levelling hills and consolidating terrace fields into larger "mini-plains" (83). In stationary mechanization, the number of motor-pumps was to be increased considerably and great emphasis was placed upon the multiplication of small, localized power-generation equipment which subsequently would permit full electrification. A leader in this field is the often-cited Yongshun Xian in Fujian, where small-scale electrification has made excellent progress. The rural industrial sector of Fujian, starting with unsophisticated water wheels, developed small 15 and 25 kW generator sets, which, fully installed, will cost 1,500¥, plus 1,000 to 2,000 man-days for preparing the feeder stream and for installation. An 88 kW station, big enough to feed a small village, costs 26,000 ¥, a sum that a brigade can raise and amortize in two to five years, after which an annual gain of 5,000 to 10,000 ¥ will become feasible. Yongchun Xian manufactures and sells such equipment after having fully electrified itself (84). It appears that this stage was by and large completed by 1975, at the end of the Fourth Plan.

The third stage is aimed at the mechanization of all areas, the completion of rural electrification and a gradual transition toward a much more capital-intensive form of agricultural production, leading to decisive increases in multiple-cropping, irrigation, yields and thereby output. For the completion of this third stage Chairman Mao had originally envisaged a period of four to five Five-Year Plans from the beginning of the entire programme, or about three after the transition from agricultural cooperation to full socialization (85). The Years of Calamity brought a certain setback, but afterwards the leadership felt that the country's economy was on sufficiently firm ground to revert to the earlier schedule.

---

83) J.H. Liu, "China Equips Her Farming Industry", Renmin Ribao, Peking, 20 June 1963.
84) Hsinhua, Peking, 16 Feb. 1976.
85) T.T. Mao, The Question of Agricultural Cooperation, Peking 1956, p.34.

Initial stage: Tractorization

Motorization began briskly during the First Plan period with the creation of the first agricultural machine and tractor stations (MTS), first owned by the State, then turned over to the xian. In 1957, there were 24,630 tractors, all imported, at work in 563 MTS, almost ten times more than the 2,720 tractors that had been available in 1953 (86). New mechanized pumping capacity amounted to 1.6 million HP. Further progress in machine use was expected to receive a decisive impetus with the coming onstream of several tractor factories which were to be built with Soviet aid during the Second Plan. The first started production in Loyang in 1958, but several others remained temporarily incomplete when the Eastern European experts were withdrawn in 1960.

The shock to Chinese expectations of attaining a meaningful degree of mechanization in fifteen to twenty years seems to have been so severe that apparently some government planners were inclined to abandon all hope of farm motorization for the time being and return to much more primitive forms of family cultivation. Policy discussions on this point reached their climax in September 1962, when the Central Committee of the CCP, in its 10th Plenum, decided to go ahead with the National Development Programme for Agriculture (87) and maintain the goal of full mechanization.

Constraints upon rapid mechanization

Examining their situation painstakingly, the Chinese authorities found constraints that are common to most developing countries. There was a dire lack, in absolute terms, of investment capital and of technology. Originally, Soviet aid was to have bridged this gap, but now China would have to provide for herself. The obstacles were overcome partly by orthodox means, i. e., investment from central budget funds to complete the unfinished plants, but also partly by specifically Chinese approaches, such as gradually building up repair and maintenance shops to the point where they could manufacture parts, then go into assembly and then into full production. This programme, which began at first in the commune sector but was later

---

86) C. Kang, Agricultural Production in Communist China, Madison, Wisconsin 1970, p.111.
87) Hsinhua, Peking, 28 Sept.1962.

shifted to the xian and diqu, was paralleled by the acquisition of the necessary technological know-how by experimentation and reverse engineering on imported foreign models.

Two later constraints were shortages of raw materials and of fuel. The gradually expanding commune steel industry slowly supplemented the large-scale State sector, to a point where the latter could limit itself to furnishing only special steels for key parts. The fuel bottlenecks gave way when China's own oil and refining capacities expanded during the 1960s.

Finally, there was a lack of demand to be overcome. The young communes were too short of capital in the years after the Calamities, their farmers were unaccustomed to the thought of working with machines, and rural labour was again abundant enough to obviate any immediate need for mechanized help. Further, in large areas topography seemed to rule out the use of machines. Again the State helped by first equipping State farms with machinery so that they could serve as demonstration units. The next receivers were collectives operating under difficult conditions, such as those in northern Manchuria or in the Huanghe flood belt of 1938 in Henan and Shandong.

Selective mechanization

From the mid-1960s onward there was no longer any doubt in the collectives that their future lay in the direction of eventual mechanization. Experience with intensified irrigation alone taught the commune farmers that the volumes of water needed to allow multiple-cropping patterns, and obtain the higher yields that the Party expected from them, could be pumped only with the help of mechanical devices. The planned hectare/horsepower ratio in irrigation, 1:1.2 in 1963 (88), had been increased to 1:2.6 by the 1970s (89), and there are many indications that it is rising still farther. Jiangsu reported in 1975 a province-wide ratio of 1:4 hp/ha (90). The diesel engines that powered the pumps had the further advantage of being multi-purpose gear capable of driving other farm machinery, such as threshers in the harvest season. In such ways it was demonstrated to Chinese farmers, who for a long time had seemed more concerned about job security

---
88) Liu, op. cit.
89) China Today, Peking, 24 Aug.1974.
90) Hongqi, Peking, November 1975.

and income, that machines were more efficient than manpower without necessarily reducing employment. On the contrary, Chinese sources insist that farm mechanization increases employment, not only by a multiplication effect transmitted through many forward and backward linkages, but also in agriculture itself thanks to intensified cultivation.

Table 8 summarizes roughly the quantitative expansion of the Chinese agro-machine park and the use of engines and electricity in agriculture.

Table 8

Mechanization of Chinese agriculture

(Total park)

Category	1960	1966	1971	Long-term target
Tractors (HP units)	ca.79,000	ca.125,000	220,000	800,000
Trucks	-	-	ca.140,000	400,000
Combine harvesters	-	-	-	450,000
Motor pumps (million HP)	1.6[92]	9	18.7	40
Electricity in farm use (billion kW)	-	2.5	5.5	16

Source: J.H. Liu, "China Equips Her Farming Industry", Renmin Ribao, Peking, 20 June 1963, and various Hsinhua Bulletins.

A good example of what has been accomplished toward rural mechanization by self-reliance is the Xiyang tractor plant in Xiyang Xian, Shanxi, a few miles from Tachai. Situated about three kilometers from Xiyang town, it belongs to the xian and was set up as a blacksmith's workshop in 1948, shortly after the county was liberated by the Red Army, to supply the town and surrounding villages with simple hand-tools. In 1958, several iron smelters were attached,

---
91) As of 1963, cf. Liu, op. cit.
92) 1958 (Hsinhua, 28 Sept.1962).

enabling the plant to make some pig iron and crude steel, but in 1963 they were excorporated and set up as a separate enterprise. The same occurred with the power-generating station created in 1959. Meanwhile, in 1961, owing to the supply crisis of the Years of Calamity, the work force was reduced from 200 to 60 workers and reverted to making hand-tools.

Beginning in 1963, the plant for a time confined its production to simple agricultural machines for which some provincial enterprises had supplied the blueprints. Subsequently, the staff was reinforced by technical specialists from Taiyuan, Changchun, and Tianjin. The production of hand-tools was turned over to a new enterprise set up nearer to Xiyang town, and from 1964 onward, the factory concentrated on five types of activities:

- manual production of threshers, degrainers, cutters and presses;

- electrical milling equipment;

- electrical irrigation pumps of two types and five capacities, ranging from 5 to 25 HP;

- simple machine-tools, such as automatic planers and grinders, to equip village workshops;

- a mechanical repair workshop for the entire xian.

Beginning in 1966, the plant started to repair, then to assemble spare parts and then manufacture entire diesel engines, the blueprints of which had been provided by a factory in Taiyuan and the Loyang Tractor Plant. In 1970, the plant was ordered to look into the possibilities of producing a small crawler tractor specifically adapted to the conditions of the North Chinese hill region. It first worked out adaptions of two tractor types, one from Loyang and the other, a hand tractor, developed in Tianjin. By early 1972, sixteen prototypes of the hand tractor and nine prototypes of the crawler tractor had been manufactured and were distributed to various communes for testing. It seems that in 1973 pre-series manufacture of the two types was begun. The caterpillar tractor, a small, sturdy model, seems to have been particularly successful. In 1975, total tractor output was said to be about 3,000 units.

In the meantime, the plant had continued its more traditional lines. In 1971, annual output had been:

410 irrigation pumps,
330 degrainers, various presses, threshers,
240 milling units,
140 machine-tools and
 56 diesel engines;

the repair shop had repaired about 33,000 different machines and vehicles. Moreover, the plant manufactured almost the entire machine and tool park with which its workers later undertook tractor production. In 1972, the work force had reached 906, and production-line techniques were introduced in 1973. The plant trained its own skilled workers and technicians in a twice-weekly evening school, attendance at which was compulsory for about 90% of the workers.

The factory obtains its steel from the nearby steel plant and foundry within walking distance, that uses iron and coal from local deposits, coal being mined within 2.5 km and iron ore within 8 to 15 km. Pig iron is produced in three older smelters, one of which, built during the first days of the Great Leap Forward, had been improved and was still in use in 1972. The two other newer smelters had replaced older ones, also erected in 1958. Their output feeds two converters, built in 1963 and 1968, with an annual output of 4,000 tons (1972). Capacity was to be expanded by 60% in 1973 by the installation of a heavier converter whose capacity was fourteen tons/day. A coking plant was under construction in 1972.

During the Fourth Plan period (1971-1975), mechanization seems to have made further decisive progress. By 1973, irrigation was being supported by stationary engines totalling more than 30 million HP (93) while in North China alone 1.5-million power wells had been sunk by 1974 (94). Tractor production was reported (95) to be reaching four times the level of 1970, which would bring it to about 200,000 units by the end of the Plan period. The rural sector had about 60,000 small and medium-sized power stations, supplying electricity to more than 70% of all the communes and over 50% of all the brigades (96).

All provinces and autonomous regions had at least one tractor production plant, most of them more than one; 97% of all xian had tractor and machinery repair shops and spare-parts manufacturing works (97). Foreign observers

---

93) Hsinhua, Peking, 15 Nov.1975.
94) Hsinhua, Peking, 12 Nov.1975.
95) Hsinhua, Peking, 14 Nov.1975.
96) Hsinhua, Peking, 10 Sept.1975.
97) Hsinhua, Peking, 10 Oct.1975.

report that tractor production totalled 100,000 heavy units and nearly 150,000 walking tractors in 1975 (98) and that total tractor output in physical units had been 557,000 during the Fourth Plan (99).

What this means in an individual province is illustrated by the case of Jiangsu, which opened one walking tractor plant in 1967, two others within the next three years, and two more since 1970. Various other repair plants went into small-scale production with an aggregate volume of 3,000 units per year. Tractor-ploughed area has quadrupled since 1965. Mechanical pumping capacity reached 3.2 million HP, and two thirds of the total arable area are now mechanically irrigated (100). In Wuxi Xian in 1975 there were almost 3,000 tractors for 800,000 mou of farmland, or one tractor or walking tractor per nineteen hectares, and one horsepower of agricultural machinery of all kinds per four mou. In Xiyang Xian the ratio was 1 HP/12 mou and in some xian of lower Guangdong 1 HP 7.5 mou (101).

In the Shanghai Municipal Region, which has always played a pilot role in agricultural modernization, 88% of irrigation and drainage and 97% of the annual workload in farming have been mechanized, making it possible to increase triple-cropping from 2% of the arable area in 1964 to slightly over 90% in 1974; the average annual increase in grain yields reached 360 kg/ha without an appreciable expansion in the agricultural labour force. At the same time, the 198 communes of the Municipal Region were running an average of 24 industrial enterprises of all sizes which supplied most of the necessary inputs (102). Similar strides were made in the field of rural electrification. Xian, communes and brigades were instructed to develop early and methodically the small and medium hydroelectric power potential of their territories. All small and medium water storage and irrigation dams are to be constructed in such a way that generating equipment can be installed subsequently. At the end of the Fourth Plan, in addition to the 60,000 small hydroelectric power stations already existing in China, it was foreseen that further development should include the installation of 5,000 to 6,000 more per year. Fully two thirds of all rural power consumption were said to have been covered from power stations in the rural sector, and it would appear that about 10% of all the

---

98) Dumont, op. cit., p.28.
99) Far Eastern Economic Review, Hong Kong, 26 Dec.1975.
100) Hsinhua, Peking, 9 Oct.1975.
101) Hsinhua, Peking, 25 Sept. and 4 Dec.1975.
102) Renmin Ribao, Peking, 18 Sept.1975.

energy generated in China comes from the commune electricity plants whose output has been said to be about 40 billion kWh a year (103).

The policy applied throughout the Fourth Plan was still one of selective mechanization, in which the initiative was left to endogenous forces within the Communes, with a view to making quick progress without disrupting the management and operational structures of the collectives. In labour deployment this implied avoiding brusque or rapid displacement of labour (104). Collectivization had now preceded mechanization far enough, and the new patterns of the commune organization were well enough rooted in the rural milieu to preclude most of the unbalancing repercussions and social polarization effects within the villages that would have arisen if any non-collective structures had subsisted. The work-point system in particular proved to be a valuable factor in maintaining a balance between those members of the communal labour force whose work was facilitated by mechanization and those whose work was not, for by separating remuneration levels from the degree of direct productivity of the function remunerated, the system does not discourage those members of the working force who have to continue working in their old manual ways. Instead, the fruits of mechanization and higher productivity are equally distributed to all those participating in collective work, and the unit income as a whole is increased, an important advantage for a community that wishes to maintain a high degree of social equality.

Meanwhile, progressive mechanization made the pursuit of private activities, such as tilling private plots, less attractive, as obviously no mechanized tools were available for them. Thus, schematically, it can be said that mechanization helps to level income differentials and social disparities from collective work within the commune and the brigades, while elements still disproportionately indulging in private sideline activities are placed at a disadvantage. Conversely, different degrees of mechanization accentuate income and wealth differentials among individual communes, and this is not only tolerated but approved by the government as constituting an incentive toward inter-communal emulation and "catching-up" movements by laggard units. Within the commune structure, the introduction of increasing numbers of machines, now predominantly maintained and operated at the brigade

---

103) Hsinhua, Peking 10 Sept.1975.
104) "The Battle to Build Tachai-tape Counties Is On", Peking Review No.76, 14 Nov.1975, p.4 et seq.

level, results in moving the economic centre of decision upwards, i. e. from the team to the brigade. Larger cultivation units and across-boundary tilling by machines suggest larger ownership units as well. This happened increasingly since 1974; land ownership was and is being transferred in many cases from the team to the brigade. Such an upward shift in ownership patterns and in economic preponderance corresponds to the government's intentions, as it promotes increasing intra-communal integration, i. e. what the Chinese call "a higher degree of collectivity". (105)

As a consequence, all reports and statements seemed to indicate that by the end of the Fourth Plan period (1975) the second stage of the three-stage programme for agricultural mechanization was well advanced if not almost completed throughout the country.

Mechanization "in the main"

As for the future, it originally appeared, in the light of Chinese statements in 1974 and early 1975, that the authorities were counting upon the forces already at work inside the communes to increase their pull effect by way of the growing manpower demands on the management and labour structure. Just as the growing diversification of tasks had led the communes from primitive manual work to the phase of farm-tool improvement and rationalization of work organization, then to semi-mechanization and the use of intermediate technology, and finally to selective mechanization and the three-way division of labour in the reformed communes, so it was expected that further increases in the manpower needs of industry, rural industrialization and rural capital construction would gradually pull agriculture into full mechanization (106).

The principal guidelines for this evolution seem to have been as follows:

The two key factors determining the rhythm and extent of the process were clearly: first, the rate of capital accumulation within the communes and xian and hence their investment potential; and secondly, the allocation of scarce resources. Financing was and is seen as primarily incumbent upon the xian, communes and, to some extent, brigades. Originally the State seems to have taken the

---

105) G.B. Ng, China's Road to Development, Equality and Full Employment, ILO, Geneva 1975, p.32 et seq.
106) Ibid., p.33.

position that if the local collectives wanted and needed mechanized equipment, they would have to adjust their own investment budgets accordingly. Furthermore, the expansion of the national industry sector was not to be unduly disturbed by the rural mechanization drive, and therefore raw materials and other inputs for the production of equipment had to come from the local and decentralized sectors. Key equipment, as for machinery factories, would, however, have to come from the State heavy industry, and the necessary provisions seem to have been made long ago. Thus the overall rhythm of progress of mechanization would still be controlled by the State planning agencies, while practical coordination would be carried out at the provincial and above all at the xian level (the xian being destined to become the main carriers of the equipment-producing industry).

This concept was so flexible that from the beginning it permitted an essentially uneven pattern of progress depending on the wide differentials in capital accumulation, natural resources, access to key inputs, technical manpower etc., between provinces and even diqu. Consequently, as the examples of Jiangxu and the Shanghai Municipal Region show, the schedule seems to have been so loose that in reality many tempos and itineraries could all be accommodated under it. The individual provinces were apparently free to set their priority targets, e.g. Jiangsu stressing all aspects of grain cultivation, Hubei (notoriously beset with problems of water conservation) giving top priority to drainage and water control, North China emphasizing rapid transplantation and harvesting by big combines, etc. This decentralized approach corresponds largely to the decentralized development strategy now in practice in all sectors and seems to have been maintained.

In a "normal" mechanized commune, the average work team seems to be destined to have at its disposal one or two walking tractors, a share in at least one bigger caterpillar tractor for earth movement, and with them a wide range of ancillary equipment, such as harvesting machines, tillers, levellers, transplanters, threshers, cutters, choppers, plant production equipment such as sprayers, etc. During most of the Fourth Plan, no definite or very close target for fulfilling these mechanization goals seems to have been in force on the commune level. Production collectives advanced as they saw fit.

Their own assessment of the situation at the transition between the Fourth and Fifth Plans, however, seems to have convinced the Chinese that another acceleration in the rhythm of development was called for. According to reports from the All-China Conference of Agriculture in the Fifth Plan in Tachai in September 1975, the authorities appeared to be dissatisfied with the prospect of merely watching the massive investments of the past five years taking their effect. These effects, although relatively slow in coming, were expected to be massive: Not only would production go up but new cultivation patterns and intensified use of inputs, which in turn would expand output and accelerate the rhythm of production, would lead to concomitant increases in overall labour requirements. Rough estimates made by the Chinese planning authorities and mentioned in the reports from the Tachai Conference, speak of a rough doubling of labour requirements during the following five years (1976-1980). This apparently was much more than had been foreseen earlier. The central planners consequently seem to have concluded that the only alternatives open for the Fifth Plan were either to forego some of the potential gains in output for which the technical conditions now existed - which was inacceptable for political reasons - , or to raise labour productivity, through mechanization, to the extent suggested by the requirement projections made by the planning authorities.

The result of all these considerations was a series of conclusions by the Tachai Conference, the second of which postulates the transition to the third phase of mechanization and its achievement "in the main" by 1980 (107). According to various statements, this implies among other things that a nation-wide average of about 70% of the main functions, such as ploughing, harrowing, planting and transplanting and harvesting, should be mechanized by that date. Significantly, this target is subordinated to the achievement of greater political awareness, socio-political consolidation at the commune and xian levels and self-reliance. The government recommends emulation of Tachai and its tested example of self-reliance in technical improvement and expansion of production, and of Xiyang Xian, the county to which Tachai belongs, in building rural industry and a strong network of technological institutions supporting agriculture. Rapid achievement of mechanization was even mentioned as one of the six goals collectives aspiring to become "Tachai units" must attain. The party organization and party cadres are called upon to animate and direct this movement. The conclusion is that qualitatively, as hitherto, rural mechanization is preceded and accompanied by socio-political transformation and integration of the rural collectives. The State again confines itself mainly to setting goals and promising assistance to those communes and xian that will find the

---

107) Hua, op. cit., p.8.

task too difficult to tackle alone. But basically, as in most cases since the Great Leap Forward, the rural collectives are directed to count only on their own forces. This could very likely mean that the xian authorities will exert greater control and pressure upon the communes with an eye both to higher accumulation rates - the praise of Tachai's higher rate of capital formation is significant in this context - and to a streamlining of investment goals and capital flows as well as attendant labour uses.

What this implies in quantitative terms is hard to say. It is not known whether the mechanization coefficients of the early 1960s (as set out in Table 8 above) still apply, or whether new land/HP, land/kW, land/tractor, etc. ratios have superseded them. From Chinese publications on irrigation, motorization and electrification of the water supply, it might be inferred that the targets have become more ambitious, and the mention of some rates attained in Tachai also suggests this. Tachai now has one tractor per nine hectares of cropland - still well below the Japanese level of one (walking) tractor to a little more than one hectare. Some foreign observers have therefore speculated that the national target may have been raised to as much as a tractor per fifty hectares as a country-wide average. Other Chinese references, such as to the land reserve still to be opened up and to the prospective aims and feasibilities of grain and cotton output, of animal husbandry, etc., imply similar upgradings in the goals for 1980. The government programme announced by Chairman Hua Kuo-feng and Vice-Premier Teng Hsiao-ping in March 1978 indirectly confirms such assumptions. According to their declarations, farm mechanization is to reach 85% of all main functions by 1985. The relatively small increase between 1980 and 1985 also seems to indicate that the government wants to leave agriculture enough time during the Sixth Five-Year Plan to iron out structural tensions and distortions which have been caused by the sharp tempo of advance during the current Fifth Plan. But the pace itself and the restatement of the ambitious goal leave no doubt that the Chinese leadership deems it feasible to have a modern, actively expanding agricultural sector by around the year 1980 - when, according to the late Prime Minister Chou En-lai, China is to possess "an all-round modern economy" in all vital respects. Chou added that China is to be in the world's top bracket both scientifically and in terms of production by the year 2000, when the country is to have joined the most advanced economic powers.

CHAPTER VIII

Conclusions

Reviewing the Chinese rural employment policies at the transition from the Fourth to the Fifth Plan, a few salient features stand out. Beyond any further doubt, China has absorbed its rural unemployment. Even underemployment has been largely eliminated as an economically relevant phenomenon. Employment, in terms of both persons actively engaged and of inputs of annual man-days and daily working hours per person active, has increased tremendously. In particular, the participation of women has been so highly intensified that even in the female sector nearly full employment has been reached. People past retirement age may still fill jobs commensurate with their strength, on a part-time basis, so that they still may earn work-points. Child labour has been eliminated, while rural youths benefit from a longer and better education, no longer entering the active work force as unskilled hands but for the most part already as semi-skilled. A far-flung adult and spare-time education network ensures that increased skills are more widely taught and constantly improved. Such overall conditions are nearly unique among developing nations.

Further, China has made great strides in cutting back the future dimensions of its labour problem by putting stringent limitations to population expansion. There is justified hope that China's future population, and hence its labour force, will cease to expand but be commensurate with the quantitative limits of the nation's natural resource endowment. At the same time, thanks to the intelligent use of available labour, China has made tangible progress toward restoring a healthy ecological balance and replenishing her renewable natural resources: soil, water, forest. The benefits of these activities are already visible, but their full impact will be felt only in years, perhaps generations, from now.

Thanks to the government's three-pronged employment strategy - with overriding emphasis upon agricultural work and subsidiary stress on employment in rural industries and rural capital construction - it has been possible not only to eliminate uncontrolled labour migration from the countryside to the cities but also to fix rural manpower in its natural environment, the village, providing employment for large labour surpluses there and thus keeping labour mobility to a minimum. At the same time, the flow of manpower reserves into urban industries, where labour demand is strong and expanding, has been regulated and is now largely limited to skilled or pre-skilled manpower and balanced with the rural economy's own need of skilled labour; it is further counterbalanced by the sustained channelling of educated and sometimes highly skilled city youths to the villages, mostly on a permanent or semi-permanent basis, and by extended working sojourns of urban cadres and specialists under a rotation schedule. Again, nothing similar is known in any other developing society.

The intra-sectoral division of functions, along with the two novel channels of mass employment - in infrastructural capital construction by mass labour investment, and in small-scale rural industry - still gives overall priority to crop work, mainly for grain production as the "key link". But increasing attention in labour deployment is attached to lines previously considered secondary, such as cash-crop cultivation, animal husbandry, small-scale aquaculture, small-scale forestry and tree plantations, and such ancillary work as the processing of agricultural produce. Thus, without removing emphasis from grain cultivation and food production or changing priorities, but thanks to the intensification of labour utilization and the horizontal and vertical expansion of land, the production substratum, China's agriculture is increasingly taking on the aspects of a well-rounded, diversified multi-culture economy.

Full employment and rising labour requirements exert increasingly strong pull effects upon labour productivity. Technological progress, initially a matter of alleviating human suffering and toil, has thus become a necessity. Increases in labour productivity are indispensable if all the tasks that China's rural economy has assumed, and objectively should be capable of carrying out successfully, are to be achieved. The major mechanization drive begun during the Third and Fourth Plans signifies in this context not a change in fundamental approach to integrated rural development but the logical continuation of strategic guidelines traced twenty and thirty years ago by the communist leadership. With the help of mechanization China's agriculture may attain the goals set for the Fifth Plan. The technological, economic and social changes it engenders are no deviation from the overall goal of creating a socialist society but rather its very concretization.

At the same time, this approach to an integrated rural development has successfully solved two other key development problems: capital substitution by other, more abundant factors; and intensified surplus generation and capital formation. Better probably than Nurkse ever anticipated, more clearly than Marx's and Engels' postulations on labour as the source of all value could ever spell out, the Chinese have demonstrated how manpower, even initially utterly unarmed and unskilled, can replace financial resources in generating fixed capital, predominantly infrastructural, and production capital. Capital formation on a grandiose scale has taken place, and is still taking place more intensely than ever, by the sheer utilization of temporarily redundant manpower.

Whether this can and will continue, however, is a different question. One would assume that China's steeply-rising manpower requirements would render the use of manual mass labour for capital construction too costly. More labour-efficient ways of executing the same projects should be found, e.g., by expanding the use of heavy earth-moving machinery. But this would run counter to the other objective of the mass labour drive: to keep up the revolutionary spirit, to educate the masses in self-reliance, abnegation and intensiveness, and to teach the young generation the value of hard physical work. The pursuit of this objective cannot be furthered by the extensive use of machinery. Here, then, two major objectives of the Chinese strategy for the reconstruction of society will clearly come into conflict, and it will be interesting to see which, as between economic efficiency and social education and motivation, will win out. In the meantime, China has gained a rural capital equipment and infrastructural network that could be the envy of most developing and even some nominally developed countries.

(The lines above were written before Hua Kuo-feng purged the so-called "radicals" and the former bureaucrats under Teng Hsiao-ping returned to a share in power. This backswing to a more moderate line may provoke a somewhat apprehensive question: Will the new Chinese regime, in the name of pragmatism, give in to the lure of production efficiency as the foremost rule of conduct in policy-making? Certain utterances ascribed to Teng Hsiao-ping suggest it, but much too little is still known about the true strategic ideas of this remarkably intelligent organizer. If it occurs, the Chinese would essentially be repeating Stalin's choice in the developmental dilemma of the U.S.S.R. in the 1920s and 1930s: they might be led to sacrifice more and more long-term goals to short-term expediency, the creation of the new society to mere economic efficiency and high outputs. This would put a stop to a highly interesting experience just at the moment when its first fruits are coming in, when the first striking results of integrated rural development have been confirmed by the facts (107a).)

Simultaneously, growing rural savings, arising out of increased material surpluses generated by intensified agricultural activity, have led to a second means of capital formation: the communal accumulation funds that permit the creation of a rural industry whose investment needs and operational financing have become largely independent of injections of capital from the centre. Capital formation and investment now proceed on parallel lines on two separate levels: the central level fed by fiscal revenue from taxes and remittances of profits from State-owned industries, permitting the creation of a modern, large-scale, centrally planned and directed industrial sector; and the local level, fed from the rural collectives' own savings and surpluses, where consumer and transformation industry, decentralized, small-scale, still often technologically inferior but rapidly advancing and autonomously expanding, is emerging. No other country in the developing world has succeeded in solving the problem of how to institutionalize the mobilization of rural private and communal savings capital and to prevent it from either leaving the rural economy or flowing unchecked into consumer-goods consumption. China's rural institutions have become financially more self-supporting and are approaching the point of being capable of fully financing the auto-expansion of the rural sector. Central fiscal funds are left for more important or more global development tasks. In other words, China's rural economy, thanks to its intensive use of manpower, the one production factor in most ample supply, has in a first stage made full use of all possibilities of capital accumulation in order to build its own industry. In a second stage, that industry is now capable of replacing the State in financing the expansion of both agriculture and its own plant capacity through socialist capital accumulation, i.e. ploughing back its profits into the rural productive apparatus.

These achievements have been made possible not so much by steady governmental guidance and intervention as by a systematic policy of downward devolution of tasks and responsibilities to lower echelons and increasingly wider

---

107a) It is somewhat reassuring that neither Teng nor Hua has thus far published major or fundamental writings that suggest a revision of basic Maoist tenets; rather they have published texts calling for improvements, review of details and moderation in practice in order to bring theory and operational procedure into closer harmony.

involvement of the lower cadre strata. With absolute emphasis on the pre-eminence of manpower and its leaders, the local rural working force has been taught to direct, implement and finance a growing array of enterprises by itself. This decentralization has gone very far in key fields of application, such as seed research, seed technology and seed multiplication, and fertilizer production, to mention only a few that have become major agricultural development bottlenecks in many other developing nations. The same approach is to be observed in the key sectors of land reclamation and improvement, water management and control, agricultural mechanization and industrialization. Everywhere the State discharges more and more of its functions upon local instances, which in turn rely upon the properly organized, sufficiently motivated and appropriately structured working force - the opposite, in fact, of the faceless host of toiling blue ants many foreigners still claim to see.

Such a strategy had a number of corollaries and consequences: one evidently is extreme politicization in conceptualizing objectives and results, another the same politicization of motivation and incentives to the labour force. A third is the isolation of the Chinese market from the impact of developments in the world market, especially external price movements, through an extensive price subvention system and the compression of Chinese imports to the absolute minimum necessary for development. Conversely, China has renounced the building of production sectors predominantly catering for external tastes and fashions and stimulating wage differentials for their work. The Chinese economy, and particularly the rural one, deliberately avoids all comparisons and competition with foreign economies in the world market - at least for the time being. International competition is not being sought while the national economy remains essentially a developing one. Therefore there is no comparison of specific performances of the labour force, whose productivity is raised only in accordance with specifically national norms, such as self-reliance, self-sufficiency, regional autarky, full employment, in deliberate disregard for competitive cost advantages. This approach has been aphoristically summarized by a foreign observer as follows: "If there is need for a commodity in a capitalist economy, one goes and buys it. In a socialist economy, one goes and manufactures it".

All this, however, leaves open some questions for the future, the Chinese answers to which are still not known: Even socialist economies are subject to the law of diminishing returns. It will cost more and more to obtain smaller and smaller increments in yield. It will cost more and more, in terms not only of financial resources but also of such scarce material inputs as steel, to pump more and more water for more multiple cropping, to open the more inaccessible stretches of potentially arable land, to exploit smaller mineral deposits for fertilizer manufacture, while labour becomes scarcer. How will China cope with rising costs and declining growth rates? How will she maintain self-sufficiency at rising per-caput consumption levels? How will she maintain the unique structure of her economy in the face of pressing needs for further rationalization? How will she resolve the potential conflict between the tenets of manual labour as an educative and mind-reforming device and the requirements of higher labour productivity? How will the social fabric, with its ideal of the essential polyvalence of most, if not all, members of the working force, stand up to the call for ever greater specialization and compartmentalization of the labour force, as is considered inevitable in a modern industrial society? And if such specialization is admitted, how will it stand up against the quest for greater equality in remuneration and social standing? Or will equality have to yield to differentiation in income, status and class consciousness as is to be observed in the U.S.S.R.? Are the great aims of the new, classless society, the removal of the "Three Great Differences" - between mental and physical labour, between agricultural and industrial work, between urban and rural living standards - reconcilable with the strains and stresses of a modern industrial society?

We do not know what concrete answer the Chinese will find for these questions, but we know that the internal debate is passionate, ardent, sometimes antagonistic, as the recent struggles between the exponents of the "revisionist line" and the "revolutionary leftists" seem to indicate. For twelve years the majority held that institutional changes have more relevance and greater scope for solutions than more technical advances (107b). One

---

107b) This was the situation approximately up to autumn 1976. The purge of the so-called "Radical" faction and the subsequent return of Teng Hsiao-ping and in his wake of a whole host of bureaucrats purged as "Revisionist" and "followers of the Liu Shao-chi line" to a share in power has again changed the context. It is likely that more pragmatism, operational efficiency and short-term expediency may gain greater ground. But nothing suggests so far that this might lead to the abandonment of policy elements that have been tested for over twenty years in the fire of often severe calamities and found well-adapted and useful.

may be sure that the Chinese answers will therefore be highly original. The Chinese thus take - and have always taken - the view opposite to that of most Western authorities on the economics and sociology of development. For the latter, the root causes of underdevelopment are lack of capital, technological stagnation, and, secondarily, unfavourable physical factors. Institutional backwardness and failure to adapt are admitted as contributing factors, but the extent of their impact is still very much in dispute. Hence, all Western development strategies concentrate their emphasis on (a) capital infusion, (b) technical transformation and, only subsidiarily, (c) limited institutional reform. If these views, especially those of the technical school, are correct, the Third World, or at least some advanced parts of it, should have made very significant progress in breaking out from underdevelopment. But the facts do not support this hypothesis.

The Chinese have held that institutional and human factors are far more decisive. They subsume under this heading - for them very significant - such aspects as national independence and political orientation. According to them, given the right politico-socio-institutional "factor mix", a situation can be created in which the initially acute lack of technological resources can be overcome, or compensated for a time until such a social momentum has been created that small, even marginal, allocations of capital and technology can engender disproportionately great changes, not only quantitatively, but eventually also qualitatively. To the sad phenomenon of "expansion without development" as it can be seen in many of the more affluent developing countries, the Chinese oppose that of a society which first changes structurally and then, deriving human energies from those societal reforms, combines material "quantum jumps" with qualitative changes from which there is no return. They further hold that their potential of institutional and societal reorganization is far from being exhausted, that "the Revolution goes on" and that only this continuing "march towards socialism" creates the really effective preconditions for the successful infusion of technological changes. The emphasis is clearly on the human factor, on changes in the attitude, motivation and organization of the labour force. One should therefore, with some exaggeration, describe the Chinese approach as a new sort of economic humanism, a "Mao humanism". The changes that have occurred in China in the last twenty-five years seem indeed to support such a view.

If the Chinese approach to development has been so successful (assuming that it really is, and to this the coming years, roughly those of the Fifth Plan, will probably furnish a better answer), and if it offers ways out of such apparently formidable bottlenecks as the persistent lack of investment capital, then why have not many countries of the Third World already adopted it? For some, the lack of comprehensive and detailed information may be an excuse. But not even those nations which take pride in calling themselves "progressive" have actually embarked upon anything as sweeping as the Chinese approach.

The reasons are given by the Chinese themselves, and above all by their foremost author on questions of integrated societal development, Mao himself. For them there can be no question of a foreign approach being slavishly copied, nor are they prepared to furnish ready-made blueprints of a home-grown model to external imitators. On the contrary, every nation has an organically grown historical sub-stratum to which all its plans must be suited. Even if Marxism in its Leninist, and now Leninist-Maoist, version offers something approaching a universally utilizable methodology, there is need for incessant and creative practical adaptation to the concrete conditions of each case. Mao himself expressed this in an unsurpassably clear passage (108):

> "Being Marxists, communists are internationalists, but we can put Marxism into practice only when it is integrated with the specific characteristics of our own country and acquires a definite form. The great strength of Marxism-Leninism lies precisely in its integration with the concrete revolutionary practice of all countries. For the CCP it is a matter of learning to apply the theory of Marxism-Leninism to the specific circumstances of China. For the Chinese communists who are part of the great Chinese nation, flesh of its flesh and blood of its blood, any talk of Marxism in isolation from China's characteristics is merely Marxism in the abstract, Marxism in a vacuum. Hence, to apply Marxism concretely in China so that its very manifestation has an indubitably Chinese character, i.e. to apply Marxism concretely in the light of China's specific characteristics, becomes a problem which it is urgent for the whole party to understand and solve. Foreign stereotypes must be abolished, there must be less singing of empty, abstract tunes, and dogmatism must be laid to rest; they must be

---

108) T.T. Mao, Collected Works, Peking 1960, Vol.II., p.196.

replaced by the fresh, lively Chinese style and spirit which the common people of China love. To separate internationalist content from national form is the practice of those who do not understand the first thing about internationalism."

The message is thus clear: the methodology is Marxism-Leninism, but it can supply only the general guidelines for the dynamic transformation of a society. The remainder, in fact by far the much larger portion, of the task is to apply this universally valid tool to the concrete conditions of each nation, or in different terms, to make a creative, living adaptation to concrete reality. China has made it, thanks to Mao's insight, and this adaptation is what Maoism is largely about. At this point, it is easy and certainly legitimate to replace the term "Marxism" by "development strategy" (after all, is not Marxism-Leninism the analytical instrument that applies historical and dialectic materialism to the problems of transforming society?), and this yields the Chinese' own formula for socio-economic development: the creative, daily-repeated application of Marxist methodology to the concrete historical and material situation of each country.

Therefore, there can be no exportation of the Soviet model or the Chinese model or any other model, like prefabricated parts of a pre-designed edifice. Such an approach would be grotesque, and suggestions in this sense made by foreign visitors have been met in China with ironic smiles. For India, for example, there can be no real question of "following the Chinese line" or "applying the Chinese model" except if this means elaborating a genuinely Indian, indigenous way of using Marxism-Leninism within the concrete Indian reality. The Indian Marxists have so far failed to do so, and in Chinese eyes this is one of the main reasons for their failure to make any major progress. To follow Mao's line in its true meaning would consequently imply not looking to China and slavishly copying Chinese inventions, but turning resolutely to one's own indigenous society and finding within it the framework for authentic solutions.

Still, from the outsider's viewpoint it cannot be denied that the Chinese did come up with some striking solutions to general, universal problems common to the entire Third World, which could, mutatis mutandis, be transposed, as will be seen below. Furthermore, the plight of the underdeveloped nations has by now reached such a point that after the failure of a quarter-century of ineffective development formulas some vigorous new outside impetus would be more than beneficial. Moreover, not all developing societies have at their disposal the enormous cultural and human resources that the Chinese nation could fall back on after Liberation. They will have to borrow from abroad. Here China offers the one case of a successful developmental take-off based not primarily on industrialization but on agricultural development, on rural diversification. Hers is the sole case where the classical approaches to capital formation and investment have been replaced on a large scale by alternative paths, where material factors have been constantly and deliberately adjusted in perspective and the human, voluntaristic factor successfully moved into the focus of all national efforts (108a).

A look at the central problem of contemporary agricultural rehabilitation, the struggle for higher yields, tellingly illustrates this point: China did not fall into the technological euphoria of the Western-induced "Green Revolution" of the late 1960s, never believed in a shortcut that could obviate hard human labour, elude the social struggle between classes, produce a cornucopia of rural wealth merely by applying massive doses of a pre-composed input package which the industrialized countries promised to contribute (and, incidentally, largely failed to deliver, at least in sufficient proportions and at price levels within the reach of the vast masses of small farmers in the Third World). India, less critical, succumbed to this restricted type of mere "seed-and-fertilizer revolution" and had to pay for it by several years of harvest failures which drove home the lesson of the absolute need for simultaneous institutional reform among the rural population. It therefore spoke well for the seriousness and integrity of Mrs. Gandhi's government that, if belatedly, it began in 1974/75 to press for land

---

108a) In May 1978, this seems to be changing. The new Hua-Teng leadership seems to eschew the voluntaristic outlook and more revolutionary approach of the Cultural Revolution. But it is too early to gauge how far they will go. It certainly may be beneficial if the unconditional, sometimes even hysterical attitudes of the last ten years, always eager to "throw out the baby with the bath water", are toned down and give place to a pause for consolidation. But would Hua and Teng be able to fall back upon this safer line, with its stress upon economy, efficiency, better material conditions and more orthodox practices, without the tremendous voluntaristic efforts of the period 1958-1976? Only the future will tell how the Chinese themselves will judge this period in retrospect.

holding ceilings, land distribution, collective amelioration projects, for freeing bonded labour from its legal fetters and for other social reforms, provoking a response without which Indian farmers could never have made the quantitative jump in grain output which pulled the country out of its worst-yet food crisis after the 1974 summer harvest. (It is true that exceptionally plentiful monsoons in 1975 and 1975/76 were instrumental in bringing human efforts to fruition.)

Consequently, it may be legitimate to ask which part of the Chinese experience is really transposable, in what form it would be transferable, what would be replicable under different conditions, so that other developing countries could benefit from those of China's accomplishments that are politically and systemically neutral.

There is probably little doubt that some well-defined, relatively easily identifiable examples could be replicated, such as applications of agricultural engineering at the intermediate level. The mechanical rice transplanters, the simple waterwheels, the methods of pre-planting and transplanting other grains but rice would be cases in point. But a broader generalization of this concept, with its emphasis on the use of home-bred inventions, would present considerable social and conceptual problems. In highly stratified societies, this would touch upon very significant individual and social interests. Learned administrators and managers would have to step down from pedestals of authority and dirty their hands and muddy their shoes along with the common people - a mortal danger in societies where the concept of "face" predominates. Foreign-trained sahibs would have to learn from peasants with calloused hands, whereas all their education teaches them to look for more and more sophisticated gadgets of imported technology. That would imply an iconoclastic attack of considerable dimensions upon a firmly set and sustained conception of the world and its values. Such a deliberate smashing of images and formulas of great prestige requires above all a political will and sustained political and ideological support and justification, including self-justification, for those who do the smashing. In the last essence, therefore, the political question is the overriding one.

Similarly, the use of unemployed labour in the slack season or the use of food wages in lieu of cash would soon raise fundamental problems of remuneration, of performance evaluation, of profitability, of surplus-value appropriation, in brief, of the entire rural property and revenue structure. Further problems would be created by the adoption of such theoretically unassailable concepts as the superimposition of larger unit structures over more basic ones, or decentralized production planning. At every turn in the passage from the platform of principle to that of concrete application, problems are encountered that in the last analysis are those of property systems, of power structures, of a political order.

Similarly, the Chinese framework of the cadre apparatus at the lowest level, the Xiafang system of "sending down" technicians and managers, the whole variegated panoply of technical capacities at the village level, are based upon a given political order that ensures unconditional implementation, even in the absence of material rewards. But how could India, for example, bring her educated youths from the cities with their glitter, their shops, their cinemas, and even their unemployment, back to the villages with their boredom, their drudgery, their incomparably lower wage scales (even if employment is assured), except by changing her fundamental values? The Chinese system consciously makes political motivation the centre of all considerations, makes the appeal to political discipline the fly-wheel within society for the tasks of development. How can systems that deliberately eschew political motivation, that know only material rewards as incentives and the good life, full of consumer amenities, as foremost aim of all activities, bring about the inevitably arduous return to the village by their trained and skilled élites? There have been some attempts along these lines, such as that of the animateurs ruraux in the Ivory Coast and other French-speaking West African countries. The animateurs were to teach and lead the villagers, but soon the experiment failed, for in the absence of a generally accepted and practised ideology they did not know what to animate their pupils with. When they read them pamphlets issued by ministries in the capital, they themselves could only see too well the unbridgeable gap between reality and general social theory. The "brain drain" did the rest.

Again, small-scale industries are now accepted from the technical viewpoint. In China they essentially depend on the savings-generating capacity of their parental communes. If, however, small-scale industries, perhaps in Africa, are to be financed from the State budget because local communities simply do not have the organs and incentives to bring out the villagers' savings and to mobilize their labour, then the exercise is to a large extent pointless, for in such cases modern full-scale industries are more cost-efficient. Similarly, country after country that had made ambitious plans for land and water management had to abandon them or scale them down to relatively insignificant individual proportions, because the resistance of vested interests could not be broken, capital was lacking, manpower mobilization on a larger scale failed and the general political will to apply decisions already taken weakened at the top.

This raises another salient point. Even if the strength of the central government was overtaxed, why could the basic labour units not pursue under their own steam the projects once started? The answer in all cases, from India to Egypt, from Senegal to Indonesia, is that even in the best circumstances, governments were and are still accustomed to plan and work <u>for</u> the people but not <u>with</u> the people. The rural population remains in a state of infantile passivity, no doubt partly because most governments, unless they are truly revolutionary, consciously or unconsciously shrink from fully mobilizing the mute, illiterate masses which they see more as a danger than as a support. Furthermore, by what methods, in the name of what, could they set the labour force into motion even if they wished to? India's Congress Party, union of the local notables <u>par excellence,</u> was in immediate danger of falling apart whenever the top attempted to animate the landless poor (109). But without active participation of

---

109) This is exactly what happened. As soon as the Union leadership under Mrs. Gandhi made a move towards putting into greater practice the lofty promises of the Congress Party, especially Mahatma Gandhi's social precepts, e.g. on the integration of the out-castes, large segments of Congress went into open mutiny, as in 1969. Later on, when Mrs. Gandhi's government finally took drastic steps towards such long-overdue policy aims as birth control, the imposition of landholding ceilings, the freeing of bonded labour, the abolition of dowries, more stringent social controls of landlords and local "capitalists", taxation of the moneyed classes and the other measures introduced from spring 1975 onward, Congress simply broke apart. The majority - even the self-appointed leaders of the Harijans, the out-castes, - went over and joined the right-wing opposition in a strident campaign against Mrs. Ghandi, alleging that "democracy in India was being strangled". Nothing could be further from the truth. For the first time, democracy had been put to work. But the smear campaign succeeded, Mrs. Gandhi was defeated in the 1977 elections, and under the new Janata coalition government everything is back to the old order - many speeches and no progress - and certainly no betterment for the oppressed rural poor.

that majority of the population there can be no decentralized planning, no local decision-making, no initiative towards self-help, no self-reliance, only indolent waiting for the government to "do something".

There are other aspects that touch even more profoundly at the nerve of the old society. All practical experience in the Third World suggests that as long as individual profit-seeking is not eradicated, there will be no real mutuality. As long as the spirit of individual competition and enrichment survives, cooperatives will probably founder or be turned into vehicles for increasing the gains of the local moneyed class, as has occurred in India, Pakistan and many Latin American countries. Thus, in its fundamental structures the Chinese model always collides with the crucial questions of class relationships, of antagonisms of interest and therefore with the tenets of the consumer society, competitive economy, the dynamism of profit-seeking and profit-making, in brief, the market economy, or as the Marxists put it, capitalism. Hence, no real adaptation of the Chinese model, even in part, is conceivable so long as clashes of major principles and outlooks are not resolved.

If, however, the Chinese approach reaps more domestic successes, if the Chinese can show that their system is apt not only to accelerate the socio-economic take-off process but to bring to what had been a severely depressed rural society the material advantages of an enlightened affluence, if at the same time the free play of market forces fails to produce significant progress in the Third World, then the Chinese way may become a serious alternative inspiration that may one day unhinge the entire established social order of the underdeveloped nations. This, in turn, would have considerable repercussions upon the economic well-being of the developed nations, whose predominant position in the world cannot be maintained if the Third World changes its camp. And this is why it is most important for the Western world to know what the Chinese do for and with the labour force - their own, immense one, and by the contagion of their example, the tremendous forces lying latent in Asia, Africa and Latin America.

BIBLIOGRAPHY

Bettelheim, C., Charrière, J. and Marchisio, H.: La Construction du Socialisme en Chine, Paris 1965.
Bettelheim, C.: Cultural Revolution and Industrial Organization in China, New York 1974.
Buck, J.L.: Land Utilization in China, Chicago 1937.
Chao, K.: Capital Formation in China, Los Angeles 1974.
Chao, K.C.: Agrarian Policy of the Chinese Communist Party 1921-1959, Bombay 1960.
Ching, T.M. and Ching, K.K.: "A Glimpse of Forestry in China", in Journal of Forestry, no.71, July 1973, London.
Corrigan, P.: "China: Socialist Construction as Thought Reform", in Journal of Contemporary Asia, London 1974, vol. 4, no.3.
Dawson, J.: Communist China's Agriculture, New York 1970.
Doak Barnett, A.: Communist China and Asia, New York 1960.
Dumont, R.: Chine: La Révolution Culturale, Paris 1976.
Eckstein, A. et al.: Economic Trends in Communist China, New York 1964.
Franck, A.G.: On Capitalist Underdevelopment, Bombay 1975.
Gittings, J.: How to Study China's Socialist Development, in IDS Communications No.117, London 1976.
Henle, H.V.: Report on China's Agriculture, FAO Rome 1973.
Ho, C.: Harm into Benefit: Taming the Haiho River, Peking 1975.
Hsin, H.W.: Tachai, Standard-bearer in Agriculture, Peking 1972.
Kang, C.: Agricultural Production in Communist China, Madison, Wisconsin 1970.
Khan, A.R.: Distribution of Income in Rural China, ILO Geneva 1976.
Kojima, R.: "China's Indigenous Technology", in Technology and People, pt. I and II, Washington 1972.
Kuo, L.T.: The Technical Transformation of Agriculture in Communist China, New York 1971.
Lippit, V.C.: Land Reform and Economic Development in China, White Plains, N.Y. 1975.
Mao, T.T.: Selected Works, Peking 1960 et seq.

Ng, G.B.: China's Road to Development, Equality and Full Employment, ILO Geneva 1975.
Orleans, L.: Every Fifth Child, The Population of China, London 1972.
Orleans, L.: "Problems of Manpower Absorption in Rural China", in The China Quarterly, London, July 1961.
Pang, T.: Les Communes Populaires Rurales en Chine, Fribourg 1967.
Reynolds, C.G.: "China as a Less Developed Economy", in American Economic Review, vol. 65, no. 3, Washington 1975.
Richardson, S.D.: Forestry in Communist China, Baltimore 1966.
Richman, B.: Industrialist Society in Communist China, New York 1969.
Segal, R.: The Crisis of India, London 1962.
Selden, M.: The Yenan Way in Revolutionary China, Cambridge, Mass. 1971.
Sigurdson, J.: "Rural Industrialization in China", in U.S. Congress, China: A Reassessment of the Economy, Washington 1975.
Sigurdson, J.: "Rural Industry - A Traveller's View", in The China Quarterly, no.50, London 1972.
Stavis, B.: Making the Green Revolution, Ithaca, N.Y. 1974.
Tawney, R.: Land and Labour in China, New York 1930.
Tuchman, B.: Stillwell and the American Experience in China, 1911-1945, New York 1972.
Tseng, W.C.: China's Socialist Industrialization, Peking 1958.
Ullerich, C.: "China's GNP Revisited", in Journal of Contemporary Asia, London, vol.3, no.1, 1973.
Wheelright, E.L. and MacFarlane, B.: The Chinese Road to Socialism, New York 1971.
U.S.Congress, An Economic Profile of Mainland China, Washington 1968.
Willmott, W.E. (edit.): Economic Organization in Chinese Society, Stanford 1972.
Wu, S.Y.: "A Report on the Chinese Commune", in Chinese Economic Studies, vol.VIII, no.3, White Plains, N.Y. 1975.
Wu, Y.L.: An Economic Survey of Communist China, New York 1956.